OPEN THE DOOR TO GIS

Teacher's Edition

TONI FISHER

loca+e
PRESS

Credits & Copyright

Open the Door to GIS
Teacher's Edition

by Toni Fisher

Published by Locate Press LLC

Direct permission requests to info@locatepress.com or mail:
Locate Press LLC, PO Box 671897, Chugiak, AK, USA, 99567-1897

Editor   Gary Sherman
Cover Art   Madelaine Dingwall
Interior Design   Based on Memoir-LaTeXdocument class
Publisher Website   http://locatepress.com
Book Website   http://locatepress.com/odg

Contents

Foreword to Teachers

Why should you use this book in your class? Why teach Geographic Information Systems (GIS) to your students? Imagine being able to add technology to your classroom easily, to enable students to learn to work with technology, not simply use it, and to be able to assess student progress in a comprehensive, efficient way. Imagine your students having fun learning, enjoying their time working with a software program that rewards their efforts with visually pleasing graphics while they are guided by stories that they will find interesting to read. *Open the Door to GIS* aims to fulfill these goals. You'll wonder why everyone doesn't add GIS to their class!

Open the Door to GIS acknowledges that many students are familiar with playing computer games. Working with GIS, through the interactive stories that shape each lesson, will seem quite familiar to students because it resembles the framework of a game. Research has shown that playing computer games is enjoyable because players get instant feedback, have a sense of autonomy, are given a sense of purpose and are engaged by the story. Just as with a game, GIS software responds instantly when icons and menus are clicked, giving positive, instant feedback. To fulfill the purpose given by the story surrounding each chapter, learners gain autonomy, being free to choose and design different ways to execute the assigned tasks. In addition, developing creativity in an interdisciplinary fashion allows students to develop functional software and technology literacy which can be used both in and outside the classroom. Just as in playing a game, *Open the Door to GIS* makes learning GIS fun.

GIS is a technology that incorporates the learning of multiple skills including graphic design, analysis, data visualization and spatial literacy, while fostering the use of a software application that has become an integral part of 21st century jobs in both government and business. GIS is not just an addition to geography classes, it can be added to almost all social sciences, arts, and sciences, as well as computer studies. Learning on such a platform, with the opportunity to excel in this variety of elements, encompasses a broad spectrum of learning styles and interests—it does more than just teach about mapping and software, it teaches *Higher Order Thinking Skills*. *Open the Door to GIS* introduces GIS to students, allowing them to explore the world in an entertaining way—it's not the usual step-by-step software instruction manual.

This book takes an approach to learning that includes several methods, underpinned by Constructivist philosophy. To the student, the most important element may be the story. To the teacher, it may be Concept Mapping. A description of all three components, Constructivism, Storytelling, and Concept Mapping, as they pertain to *Open the Door to GIS*, follows.

A suggested curriculum-mapped timeline for study is given, as are links to resources needed to set up the classroom. Notes for teaching each chapter are included.

Look forward to enjoying GIS with your class this semester! Watch your students develop their skills and their confidence with software.

Storytelling

Using a story for teaching is an ancient method that has been perpetuated through civilisations because it is such an enjoyable and effective way to learn. People, regardless of age, like stories. When being told a story, people relax and listen, causing them to be more receptive to the transfer of information. Stories capture our attention and the information conveyed is learned more readily.

Stories are compelling because they use multiple areas of the brain. They use sensory specific words and emotions that increase the creation of personal attachment and deeper understanding needed in the permanent associations required for seamless recall. On the other hand, learning that is delivered without a story is often more difficult to recall because internal associations may not have been created. For this reason, learners often use mnemonics to assist with learning, but they are not as effective as a compelling story with a beginning, middle, and end, nor are they as conducive to an enjoyable learning experience.

Stories used in *Open the Door to GIS* undertake to engage the reader in a world where they can independently solve a problem and succeed. Along the way, their involvement with the story assists them in learning about GIS, specifically, and software in general.

Constructivism

In association with current educational pedagogy, *Open the Door to GIS* undertakes a Constructivist approach to teaching and learning. Constructivism is a philosophy of learning and teaching whereby the learner constructs their own knowledge. Learners are not passive recipients sitting in a classroom waiting for the teacher to tell them what they need to know. Instead, they are active learners, seeking knowledge as well as learning how to learn.

Teachers who are Constructivists are guides to learning. As a guide to learning, a Constructivist teacher must be careful not to become a leader. When learners think that a teacher knows everything and they, themselves, are less powerful, they look to the teacher to do the work for them, making the suggestions and solving the problems, instead of developing personal competency. If a teacher will solve their problems when they raise their hands, they are more likely to raise their hands before they think for themselves. They will not become independent learners.

Constructivist teachers of GIS need to resist the innate desire to take charge by giving an answer. This can be the most difficult element of Constructivism: to not give an answer, to let the answer be discovered. Teachers need to let the students find their own way through the software menus and tools and let them solve problems using their own methods. Everyone's approach may be different, but no one's approach will be wrong. Software evolves and changes. We are all exploring the best way to do things. Creating new methods leads to the creation of new solutions. A Constructivist teacher will encourage the learners to be creative problem solvers, to explore, not to be followers of any one solution currently being used. For teachers who are new to teaching with or about technology, *Open the Door to GIS*, will provide a way to get started—a way for the class to learn together.

For deep learning to occur, students need time to reflect on what they have seen, heard, or read. Reflection is a key element in active learning. If students are only recipients, are only listening to what the teacher has already taken the time to learn, they are less likely to retain the information. Constructivist teachers need to ensure that enough time is given to students to discover solutions. It is more important to understand what is being taught, and why, than it is to be able to memorize vast amounts of unconnected information or to be able to follow procedures by rote. Constructivist teachers will give students tools and tasks and then wait to see how they will use them.

Learning is messy, difficult, hard work, but messy, difficult, hard work is the most rewarding kind. On the other hand, being told what to do and how to work is relatively easy, but it is a shortcut that does not result in the deep learning that students will need as they progress in their education. Students who are used to being told what to do and how to do it, will initially resist Constructivist methods. When learning new things, frustration often occurs. Students will ask the teacher to fix their problems. If the teacher knows how and offers the answer, the student will be able to follow the instruction, but the student will have missed out on the satisfaction of solving the problem for themselves. Initially students may try to solve a problem, repeatedly using the same method, and becoming increasingly frustrated. Eventually, if left to their own devices, they will seek to solve the problem in another way, methodically, by accident, or with lateral thinking. After the frustration, the rebound of their self-esteem, from their success, will be much more rewarding than the reward to which they may be accustomed, that of simply having been able to complete the exercise, having being told what to do.

Using *Open the Door to GIS*, a Constructivist teacher will read the stories and skim through the instructions. By not doing the exercises ahead of time, by not being an expert, the teacher will be better equipped to let the students learn through Constructivist methods.

Remember, victories are the result of a struggle. Provide your students with an opportunity for victories by not providing them with an easy answer.

Concept Mapping

If you haven't used Concept Mapping for your own learning and for teaching, you are in for a treat. Concept Mapping is increasingly popular in all levels of learning and has been the focus of significant research. Having a quick search online for some images of Concept Maps, or images of how to teach Concept Mapping, will give you a graphic introduction to Concept Maps and Concept Mapping, and may even inspire you to start reading the literature about it.

Briefly, a Concept Map starts with a central concept, connected by lines to other concepts, categories, and subcategories. A good way to start teaching about Concept Maps is to give students a skeleton map, a list of words they should incorporate into their diagram, as is done in the first chapter of *Open the Door to GIS*.

Although there is no right or wrong way to create a Concept Map since they reflect personal learning, it is easy to see if a student has missed connections, or misconnected elements. The more connections in a Concept Map, the more sophisticated the student's understanding is likely to be. Assessing students' progress becomes quick and easy. It is important to remember that students are likely to start and finish at different stages and levels of understanding based on their previous knowledge. The progress between their first map and their last map is what should be assessed.

Concept Maps should grow as knowledge grows. With Concept Maps, students no longer learn facts by rote; they learn concepts that have connections to what they already know and learn to associate the new facts with new connections.

Students can create Concept Maps with paper and pen, or use software such as PowerPoint or Inkscape, a free, multiplatform application. Using software might be preferable since it allows for the students to move concepts and create connections without having to erase and rewrite and to resize the font as the Concept Map becomes larger. If you are using a tool such as PowerPoint, you will need to ensure that students know how to create a text box and to use shapes (arrows and/or lines).

Completed Concept Map examples for each chapter are included below.

Timeline and Teaching Suggestions

Open the Door to GIS encompasses a semester of learning, for three to four hours per week for the eleven chapters. A suggestion for the breakdown of the time is to allow for one lesson to read, explore, and perhaps begin the activity. To give time to reflect on the topic before the next lesson, having a break between the first and second lessons of the weekly topic, is desirable. In the second lesson, the students will do the activity that follows the story. In the third lesson, they will review their work and work with their Concept Maps. For a final lesson, they might talk about what they have done, in groups, or in whole class discussion/show and tell.

Different learners may proceed at different speeds and show inclination to spend more or less time with particular elements or chapters. This is an introductory level course where any learning is valuable. Learning how to learn software, learning about GIS, and learning to learn with confidence are all goals, but they all take time and each learner will proceed at their own pace.

You know your students. If you think it might help incentivize them, consider giving them awards such as *Most Creative Map*, *Most Creative Solution* or *Most Colourful Work* at the end of each chapter. Alternatively, having students work as a group for the awards might encourage them, through a sense of responsibility to their team, to do more than simply complete an exercise—to fully explore what can be done if different options are investigated.

There are a lot of files created in GIS. Keeping a file structure, with one folder per chapter may assist students. They should save their work to the chapter folder and it will include a Concept Map, GIS data files, and a Project File.

For grading purposes, a Concept Map for each chapter should be completed and saved. It will form the foundation for the next chapter, but should not be overwritten. A Project should also be saved for each chapter. You may want to have printed maps as well, if facilities permit.

What to do before the class starts

Download and install QGIS on all computers, creating an icon on the desktop. Download the manuals (training manual and tutorial material and put them on the desktop.

- QGIS Site `http://www.qgis.org/en/site/`

- QGIS download software `http://www.qgis.org/en/site/forusers/download.html`

- QGIS training manuals `http://docs.qgis.org/2.14/pdf/en/QGIS-2.14-UserGuide-en.pdf` `http://docs.qgis.org/2.14/pdf/en/QGIS-2.14-QGISTrainingManual-en.pdf`

- If desired, install software for creating Concept Maps. Inkscape can be found at `https://inkscape.org/`

Chapter Contents

Chapter One: Open the Doors and Look Inside

This chapter introduces a way to approach learning, a metacognitive strategy for the software, and also for learning in general. Rather than assisting the students with learning content, this chapter is aimed at assisting them with a strategy for learning how to learn, using QGIS software as an example.

In the story, a new student starts school and is overwhelmed by a new house, new bus, new school, new classroom, and new people. She reflects that the many new doors she opens on her first day are like the many items and tools that can be opened in the software program she will be learning. Her new teacher helps and encourages her with the introduction of learning strategies including active learning and Concept Mapping.

Sample Concept Map for Discussion and Grading

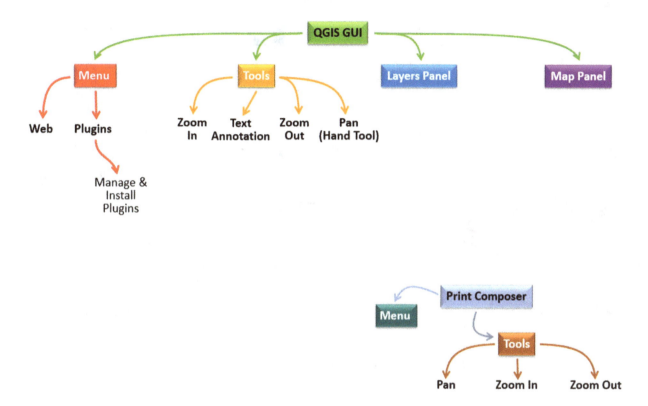

Figure 0.1: Concept Map - Open the Doors

Student discoveries for this chapter may include:

- The GUI, the graphic user interface, and the print composer are two different entities. Later the students should discover the tie between the two.

- The GUI has elements that open up hierarchically. The top-level elements have subelements, which have subelements of their own.

- The Print Composer is the same, but with different elements and subelements.

Chapter Two: Come to My Party

This chapter will allow learners to approach the software from a holistic point of view. The goal is for the learner to get the big picture with an easy win—creating a satisfying product.

The writer of the chapter is going to have a party. The way for a person to get invited is to create a map showing where they come from or where they want to go in life and to bring the map to the party as their invitation.

Sample Concept Map for Discussion and Grading

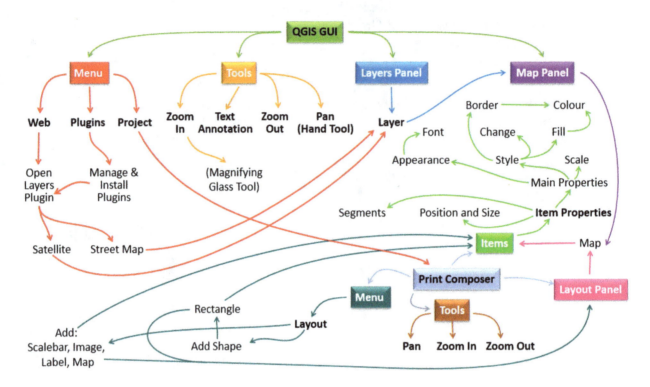

Figure 0.2: Concept Map - Come to my Party

Student discoveries for this chapter may include:

- Print Composer has elements and subelements, just as the GUI does, but they affect Layouts in Print Composer, not Maps in the GUI. For example, one can Zoom In on a Layout without changing the Map in the GUI, whereas if one Zooms In on a Map in the GUI, the Layout in Print Composer is affected.

- Students should recognize that the map in the GUI is the same map as the one in the Print Composer.

- Item Properties are specific to Print Composer.

- Different Items have different properties associated with them.

- Print Composers are associated with Projects in the GUI and are saved with them.

- Plugins may install under Menu items. Later students will see that they can also be installed as Tools.

Chapter Three: Freedom

This chapter will allow learners to begin to work with data by creating their own interpretation of the requirements. Since the data is their own creation, they do not have the added complication of worrying whether the data elements are correct or incorrect; they can focus on the process. Exploration and creativity are to be commended.

The story features a rabbit who is overly proud of its tail and because of that, is nearly eaten by a fox. How does the rabbit escape? The reader is invited to apply for a job, by the rabbit, who wants a record of the achievement to show off to the other rabbits.

Sample Concept Map for Discussion and Grading

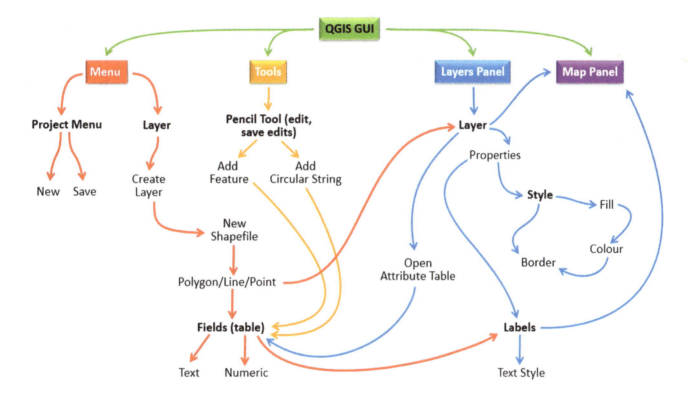

Figure 0.3: Concept Map - Freedom

Student discoveries for this chapter may include:

- Shapefiles can be of type Point, Line, or Polygon.

- Shapefiles have an Attribute Table which can be opened from the Layer.

- The Attribute Table holds the geographic location as well as descriptive attributes, including text and numeric items.

- The geographic location field is a hidden field since users do not create it.

- There is a function that creates Fields (columns) in the Attribute Table to show location, if it is required. The student is not asked to do this, but may want to research it.

- In Edit mode, Features can be added to Shapefiles by clicking on the map. This adds a row to the Attribute Table.

- In Edit mode, Fields can be added to Attribute Tables.

- The Map Panel is a display of Layers. Layers are added to the Layers Panel when, for instance, a new Shapefile is created.

- A Layer is a graphic display of, for instance, a Shapefile. Later the students will work with other data formats that can be added to the Layers Panel.

- Layers have Properties. One of the Properties is Style. Style can be used to symbolize data.

- Labels, based on the data in a Field, can be displayed on the map through Properties: Labels.

- All Features and Labels have Styles so that colour, thickness, border, fill, size, etc. can be changed for display purposes.

Chapter Four: Treasure Hunt

This chapter will allow learners to add to their skills in digitization of data, this time using a different method of data creation.

A library book with a treasure map scrawled in the margin is discovered. To find the treasure, the map must be created following the directions given.

Sample Concept Map for Discussion and Grading

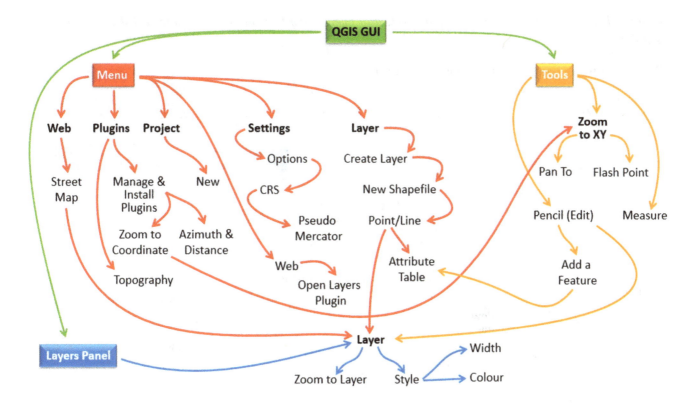

Figure 0.4: Concept Map - Treasure Hunt

Student discoveries for this chapter may include:

- Plugins sometimes install under Menus and sometimes become Tools.

- Different tools and plugins have different sorts of menus and tools associated with them.

- Maps can be of type Geographic or Projected.

    - Geographic is based on Latitude and Longitude on a globe.
    - Projected maps distort the globe into a flat surface.

- All maps have X and Y coordinates describing their position on the map with X being along the bottom of the map and Y going up the side. The coordinates are shown in the Task Bar at the bottom of the GUI.

Chapter Five: Just Give it a Try

Mapping is as much an art as a science. Some people excel in one form of expression, others in another. This chapter gives students with artistic abilities the opportunity to explore maps as art. For the less artistic, it provides a way to be creative using graphic design templates. For both it allows them to think through the process of creating a map to illustrate information.

A student tries to win a prize by using GIS when a teacher tells the class: *"There is a fantastic opportunity for one of you, one very hard working and lucky student, to travel to a technology fair during the school break. All costs, travel, accommodation, food, and even entry to some extra events, will be covered by the scholarship."*

Sample Concept Map for Discussion and Grading

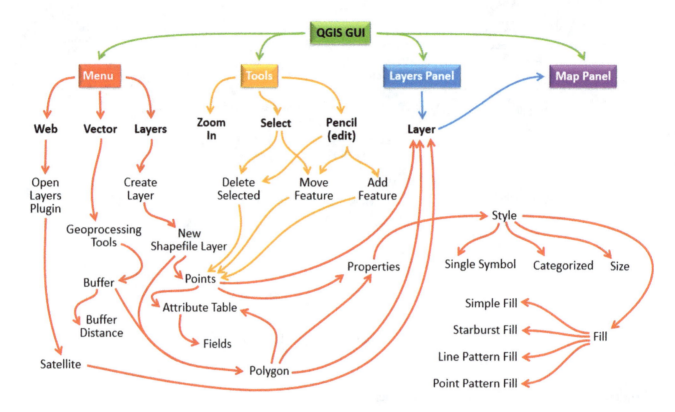

Figure 0.5: Concept Map - Just Give it a Try

Student discoveries for this chapter may include:

- Shapefiles can be edited by clicking on the map. Editing includes adding Features, moving them or deleting them.

- Buffers are Polygon type Shapefiles created from existing Shapefiles.

- Features can be drawn all the same way, with a Single Symbol, or can be Categorized, based on Fields in the Attribute Table so that they draw differently although they are one Shapefile.

- QGIS Symbology is very rich. If students take the time, they can discover a plethora of methods to illustrate their data.

Chapter Six: Flight Path

This chapter follows on the use of buffers from the previous chapter with focus on the source of the data for creating buffers.

A flock of geese is heading south but it needs a new map to get there, past the cities and the hunters. The map creators will map the cities and work with data to communicate using Nominal, Ordinal, Interval, and Ratio methods of classification.

Sample Concept Map for Discussion and Grading

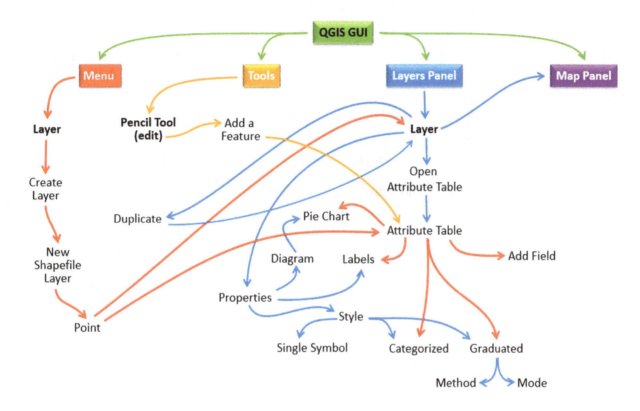

Figure 0.6: Concept Map - Flight Path

Student discoveries for this chapter may include:

- If students want to show the same information in different ways, perhaps to assist with analysis, Layers can be duplicated and then symbolized differently. There are not two shapefiles, there are two symbolizations of one shapefile.

- Choices for symbology classification methods include using:

  - Nominal (such as names of cities),

  - Ordinal (ranked order),

  - Interval (Quantiles—dividing numeric data into four equal categories, Natural Breaks—looking for breaks in the data and allowing the data to decide how the categories should be formed),

  - Ratio—percentages of data.

- Some data can only be symbolized in one way, other types can be symbolized in many ways.

- Communicating with maps is a skill dependent on picking the best communication method.

Chapter Seven: Group Work Groan

There are two predominant ways to represent data in GIS, with vectors, as illustrated in Chapters 3–6, and with rasters, the introduction to which occurs in this chapter. Group work is not always easy. Learning to work as a group is assisted when the activity instruction includes how groups work effectively, not just a focus on content. There are different philosophies for group members—to use the member's strengths or to strengthen the member's weaknesses. Groups might want to try both methods.

A group of students explores working together as they cooperate, create a map, and write the instructions for others to follow so that they can duplicate the map.

If students have an Internet connection, they can download their own raster data. Alternatively, you may want to do it for them. A good site for free raster data of the type they will need can be found at Web GIS: `http://www.webgis.com/terr_us75m.html`. You can pick a state and then a file. Each file will download quickly and can be used by one team.

Sample Concept Map for Discussion and Grading

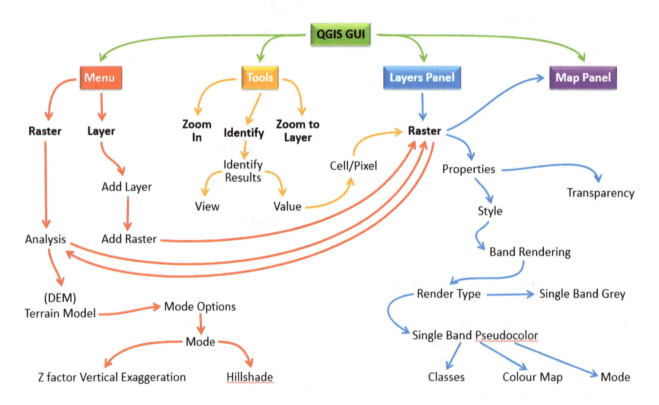

Figure 0.7: Concept Map - Group Work Groan

Student discoveries for this chapter may include:

- Shapefiles are only one kind of data. They are a type of data called Vector. Raster is another form of data that can become a Layer and be displayed in the Map.

- Rasters are grids. Each cell of the grid has at least one Attribute.

- If a Raster is black and white, it can also be Rendered as a Pseudocolour to assist with interpretation.

- If a Raster has elevation as an Attribute, it can also be made into a TIN, which emulates a 3D presentation, but in 2D Vector format.

Chapter Eight: The Magic of Mapping

Current education leans towards quantifiable data, not because it is the only kind of data, but often because it is easy to work with. There are other ways to see the world. To give opportunity to students who see the world in a different way, this chapter is aimed at separating and merging the two views of the world, the quantitative and the qualitative. Work on rasters is continued.

The student telling the story explores how to depict the world in a map, as it is personally perceived. The map is then made into a 3D perspective.

Sample Concept Map for Discussion and Grading

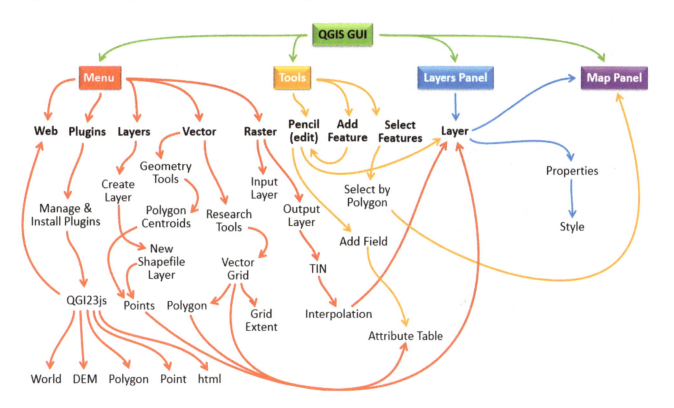

Figure 0.8: Concept Map - Magic of Mapping

Student discoveries for this chapter may include:

- Data can create data. Students can use a Point Shapefile to assist with making a Vector Grid. They can use the Vector Grid to create another Point Shapefile, this time of the center points in the Grid.

- Points with a Z value, representing elevation, can be extruded and be viewed in a browser as 3D. The 3D file created is stored on the device where it was created as an HTML file.

- The many parameters involved in creating a 3D view can be explored to allow for quite different results.

Chapter Nine: Story Map

Revisiting the process of making a map in Chapter 2, the students create a story map using the skills learned in the previous chapters and adding a few more.

Students decide on a story they want to tell. Suggestions are made for different methods by which they can present their story to the class once a story map has been created. Alternatively, they can present their stories using any way they think works best for their chosen topic.

Sample Concept Map for Discussion and Grading

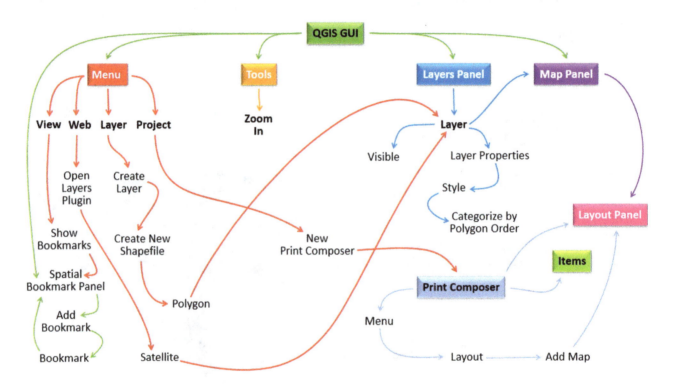

Figure 0.9: Concept Map - Story Map

Student discoveries for this chapter may include:

- Maps can be used to communicate information in many ways, not just with symbology, but also by using the functionality of the mapping software.

- Bookmarks can be used to allow easy navigation to mapped areas at a certain scale.

- Different views of maps can be amalgamated in one Print Composer.

- Shapefiles can be created to allow telling a story, piece by piece, as the story is revealed.

- If a student does some extra reading or thinks of other techniques already used, they could come up with other, different methods, such as scale dependency or toggling the visibility of layers.

Chapter Ten: GIS Quest Game

This chapter is a challenge chapter. It requires the students to use all the skills they have learned to date to create a game for a player. They put the game together while they write the instructions for the player. The basis is that teaching someone else, creating the instructions to follow, solidifies one's own knowledge.

The student is assisted with making a computer game using GIS. The premise of the game is that scientists from the future need Rare Earths to save the world. The student creates the game for another player, hiding instructions and clues within the GIS program, using different GIS skills and techniques.

Sample Concept Map for Discussion and Grading

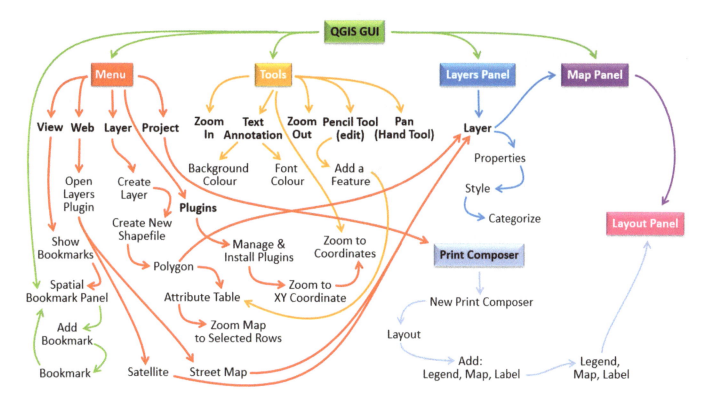

Figure 0.10: Concept Map - GIS Quest Game

Chapter Eleven: Mission Accomplished

A student talks about GIS topics for a final class presentation and discusses how open source software offers the opportunity to be part of software creation versus simply a user of software.

1. Open the Doors and Look Inside

Doors. So many doors. Some of them had looked ordinary but what was on the other side was hard to handle. Some of them seemed scary, but once opened, actually offered comfortable surroundings. Some, well, I just wasn't so sure what they held for me just yet. Let me go back to yesterday so that I can explain. . .

The rain pelted against the windows so hard we could hardly see out. It was dark, end of the day, and the end of a very long drive. I had no idea what we passed on the road after we turned off the lighted highway. Eventually Dad, who knew where we were going, slowed down and turned into a driveway. Dad jumped out of the car and opened the rusty driveway gate, shoving hard against the heavy metal. He got back in the car, drove through, jumped out again, closed the gate, and returned. He drove slowly, cautiously, aiming the lights between the black trees. As we drove, the trees shed huge drops, leaves, and twigs onto the windshield. The driveway was a morass of mud and potholes. Dad carefully eased the car through the worst of the holes. Occasionally there was no way around, so Dad eyed them up and picked the hole deemed to be less hazardous. When he guessed wrong, we all jolted and groaned as the car banged its undercarriage against the mud and gravel. Not a great start for the entrance to our new house.

Finally we stopped at the front of the house, looked up the wooden stairs and railing and across the porch to the front door, covered in strings of peeling paint. In the dark I couldn't tell what colour they were, but they weren't pretty. I looked at my brother and mother, and they looked back at me, all three of us grimacing and frowning—what were we getting into? So far only Dad had seen the new house, and his description of it did not include the horrific driveway, a porch that looked as if it might collapse, and a door that was shedding its paint in streamers.

"Right," Dad said cheerfully, "grab a case or box and run for the door. I'll unpack the rest later. Tonight we need to get inside where it is dry and be ready for some great things tomorrow."

I thought it was nice he was so cheerful, but I had reservations about anything great happening. The first day at a new school—to say I was apprehensive was a massive understatement.

In the dry of the porch, Dad fumbled for the key and opened the door. It screeched as if it hadn't been opened in decades. "Inside, inside, find a room, cuddle up," he instructed. Mum herded us upstairs in silence, ushering us through a few doors and into rooms before we found what looked to be a bedroom. I stopped in the doorway, intrigued by the huge windows surrounded by thick, velvety curtains, the wooden window seat, and the fireplace; cold, no wood, but there was potential there. "I'll take this room," I said.

My Mum and brother went on down the hall and I listened as more doors opened and closed, the sounds fading as they moved farther away. I shrugged off my backpack and put down my box. I took out my sleeping bag and laid it on the wooden floor. I was so tired that as soon as I shut my eyes, I heard nothing more until morning when Mum opened the door and told me to get ready. "The bus will be here in an hour," she announced. "It picks you up at the end of the driveway. Get dressed, have some breakfast, and go HAVE FUN!"

What was she talking about? Fun? A new school, new kids, new teacher. What was fun about that? Nevertheless, I dressed in my favourite jeans and sweatshirt before I remembered I needed to wear a uniform. Grey skirt, grey tights, grey jumper, black shoes. I looked out my window. At least the day wasn't grey, even if I was going to be. Already the sun was shining and I was a tiny bit excited to see the outside of our new house.

Breakfast done. School bag packed. My brother and I cringed again as the door screeched open. We walked down the driveway, avoiding the puddles. Near the end of the driveway, I saw a few butterflies in a patch of sunlight and smiled. Butterflies were good, maybe even a good omen. My brother threw his shoulder into it, as he had seen my Dad do last evening, and pushed open the gate. Wouldn't you know it, just then, a car went by on the road and wiped the butterfly smile right off my face with a splash of dirty water from a puddle on the side of the road, landing square onto my skirt and jumper. The car was followed by the school bus. No time to go back to the house to dry off, no time to change. I was going to my first day, wet and muddy. The door of the bus sighed open and in I went.

The bus was nearly full. My brother walked to the back and sat beside another boy who was younger than him. I took a seat right at the front beside a girl who was reading a book. She didn't look at me. I couldn't see much out the window without leaning too far into her space, but I did catch a glimpse of the field beside the road. My father said there was a shortcut through the field to the school and I could take it if I wanted to walk instead of taking the bus. The atmosphere in the bus was downright cold, freezing even, dead silent. I thought a walk through a field would be a much nicer way to travel to school. Luckily it was a short ride, we didn't pick anyone else up, and soon the school loomed in front of us. I followed the line of students into the school, through the double doors, collected my brother from the line, and walked to the door with the sign *School Administration* painted in big black letters on the opaque glass. I hated doors like that, they let in light, but you couldn't even peek in to see what was on the other side. Using the cold, metal knob, I opened the door and introduced myself to the person at the front desk. Luckily the school secretary had a friendly look and was waiting for us. Sometimes head office people were cranky and treated students as if they were annoyances. This one took us to our rooms, smiling and chatting about how glad she was to meet us.

First stop, my classroom. Outside my classroom, before she knocked and opened the door, I took a deep breath. I let go of my breath as I walked through, willing myself to be calm. I wondered what I would see and what would become of me in my new class, my new school, my new life.

Too many doors, I thought, as I stared at the table groups looking up at me. Too many doors in too little time. Too many new things behind those doors. How could I ever become comfortable with all of these changes? To say the least, it was daunting and I was overwhelmed. As I walked toward the front of the class, I decided I needed a strategy. I needed a way to approach all of the new so that I could feel comfortable and learn all I needed to know about my new life.

I sat down. The teacher started to talk. "Class, we will continue on with the software exploration today. By the end of the day, I would like you to hand in your Concept Map."

I panicked. The class was already ahead of me. I knew nothing about the task, about the software, about what was expected, about Concept Maps. I blinked back some tears and waited, letting my hair hang over my face to hide from the world. The noise of a chair beside me made me start. I turned.

The teacher smiled at me. "It must be a bit overwhelming for you today. I hear you are new to town and new to the school and now I've thrown you into the middle of an exercise the rest of us have already begun work on. You must be feeling pretty uncertain; maybe even a bit scared?" I nodded, just a bit, peeking out from behind my hair.

"Okay," she went on. "Let me fill you in a bit—but only a bit. I believe you should be doing the learning for yourself, and most importantly, the thinking for yourself. I'm just here to guide you if you get really stuck. With our kind of class and with the kind of learning we want to take place, any direction you go is just fine. You just have to pick a direction and start off on the path."

That sounded okay to me. At least she wouldn't be grading me on right and wrong for everything.

"What we are working on is this software program, called QGIS. It is a mapping program, but the map is really just one part of what the program does. You'll find out a lot more about what it is and what it does as you work with it. But, it is a big program. Open it up. Double click on the icon on your desktop."

I double clicked and waited. When it opened up I saw a lot of words, frames, and icons. My eyes widened.

"Lots of stuff," agreed the teacher when she saw my reaction. "Now what you have to do is explore. That is what the rest of the class is doing right now. First thing to think about in learning how to learn is you have to do something, not just listen to someone talk about it, or watch them do it. You have to be active in your learning. And you can do whatever you want. You can read about the program." She pointed to two icons on the screen. "That is the user manual and this is the training manual. Some people like to read and then look at the program or to follow along as they read. Other people like to just start clicking on menus and icons to see what they do. What kind of learner will you be?" she asked. "Maybe a bit of both?" I nodded.

"Remember, I said you were going to be an active learner." I nodded again. "One of the activities you will need to do is to make a Concept Map from the skeleton Concept Map I made for you."

She pointed to a document on the desktop. "You will open that document first and, after you have done some reading and exploring, arrange the words into kind of map of the program, a map of how the pieces of the program fit together." She smiled. "Funny, a map of a mapping program." I smiled back at her.

"Connect the names, the concepts, together with links. You'll find an example on the page," she explained. "Arrange and connect as many as you can. Keep on connecting and adding to the concepts as you work through all of the exercises in the days to come. Afterwards you will have a really good idea of what is in the program and how it fits together, as far as you see it. The concepts you need to add are in bold, italics, in the text. But you don't have to add only those words. This Concept Map is yours, created by you to be used by you. There is no right or wrong. Your map may not look like everyone else's, so don't compare. But if there are some things that you can't fit in or don't understand, then that needs some help and some more discussion. I want you to ask questions," she said. "But don't mistake needing to ask questions with needing to discuss your work."

I didn't understand and she went on to explain. "Look at that poster above the board."

I read: "We learn 10% of what we read, 20% of what we hear, 30% of what we see, 50% of what we see and hear, 70% of what we discuss, 80% of what we experience, 95% of what we teach others."

After I had finished reading, she continued. "We want you to be in the higher end of what you remember about the software, so we want discussion, but see if you can find the answers to your questions before you ask, otherwise you are just listening to me and being told, which puts you into the lower end, maybe the 20%."

She stood up. "Now, that is a lot to think about. Don't rush it. Give it some thought before you get started. What does what we discussed mean to you? Maybe you can write it down as you think. She smiled at me again as she walked to the front of the class. "Remember—active learning. Whatever you think is your best is going to be great."

I felt better. I was glad she gave me some time to think. She was right, I could learn to be a better learner. The program was new, and so was my life. I thought about my new house. All the doors. That was kind of like the program. All of the menus and icons opened doors.

I clicked on a few and read what was inside of them, just as I had opened up the doors to my new house to see what was there. There were lots of doors in my house and lots of things in the program, but I wouldn't know what they were about until I explored. At home, some of the doors led to interesting places I saved for later, some to places I needed right now, like my room and the kitchen. Some of the doors were hard to open and I imagined some of the program items would be harder to work with than others.

Looking at the program as a bunch of doors appealed to me. I could make a kind of map about their contents and try to make lists. Later I could see how the lists compared and could be fitted together to make things. I thought that was what she meant about the Concept Map I was going to make.

I thought about driving into my house last night and leaving it this morning. The driveway was filled with holes into which the car bumped. Likely my approach to learning the software would not always be even and easy to navigate.

A poster at home on my wall said, "Be gentle with yourself, you're doing the best you can." My aunt gave me the poster after I had a really hard time at school one day. I came home discouraged with a lousy mark on a test. The next day she took me out for cake and tea at a pretty restaurant with a window overlooking the river. Ducks and swans floated by. She gave me the poster and I read it. She asked me if I had tried hard, and I said yes, through the tears and anger I felt at the test—unfair and too hard. She reminded me I hadn't been unkind with her baby, my cousin, who was only two when she dropped and broke my favourite game. "But she's just a baby!", I protested. "Yes, she is new at learning how to handle things and you were gentle with her. Be sure you are as kind to yourself. Don't you deserve it?"

I thought my aunt was right and her poster was a good foundation for a learning strategy. I should not get angry with myself when I had trouble learning. I should be gentle. I should try the best I could and that meant to keep on trying, not to get angry, not to be defeated.

I looked down at my hands, in my lap, and saw some mud from the puddle the car had splashed over me and I hadn't managed to wipe off. It reminded me of a favourite book when I was younger where the teacher told the students to "Take chances, make mistakes, get messy." Well I was messy already. When I delved into the software it was likely to be bumpy and messy, but I had to remember to be gentle with myself, as well as to enjoy the mud that got splashed on occasion.

I wondered, is this what learning strategy is about? Thinking about my life and seeing how it worked with the rest of the things I needed to do? The teacher's poster said I would remember more of what I personally experienced. I read it again. Maybe it was right.

I thought about the rest of the things jostling around in my mind: the field where my father said there was a shortcut. Shortcuts were good, I thought, for saving time, but they might not be good for other things, like learning about the other kids who were in my new school. Hmmm—shortcuts needed more evaluation. Sometimes they might be good, sometimes not.

I thought about my fear. Fear of...? A list might be in order. What was I afraid of? If I made a list, maybe I could match the list of my fears about my new life with the fears I had about learning this software. Maybe if I could make a really good list, I would know a bit more about how to win out over the fears and get to the learning part. Where to start with that?

Doors. Which ones to open? How to open them? What would be on the other side? There was only one way to find out. I was going to start clicking and start writing, start making lists, start doing. I think that is what the teacher meant. I had to do this for myself. I opened up the document with the *Skeleton Concept Map* and got started.

You are a new student too—new to this software program. Follow the instructions given by the teacher. Do the reading. Do the clicking. Make connections on the Concept Map.

You may want to start by reading *QGIS GUI* in the User Guide and *Module: The Interface* in the Training Manual. Also look at the Glossary in this book for definitions and concepts that you will need to learn about as you work through the chapters.

You can make the Concept Map on paper, but as it grows—as you add the words in *bold, italic* throughout the chapters and others you think are important from the text, it might get messy. A digital version might be a better choice because you can move words around on a page without having to start all over again. Choose a software program that will allow you to type and draw arrows so that you can link your concepts. Starting with a font size of 14 will likely allow you to fit all of the concepts onto one map by end of Chapter 10. See the example of a Concept Map in Figure 1. Eventually your Concept Map could be huge and very complex. But remember, no two Concept Maps will look alike. The map is your own creation.

Figure 2 shows the words to use for the first edition of a Concept Map for QGIS. It will change as you go on. How can you organise and connect the concepts of this list, based on your reading and clicking?

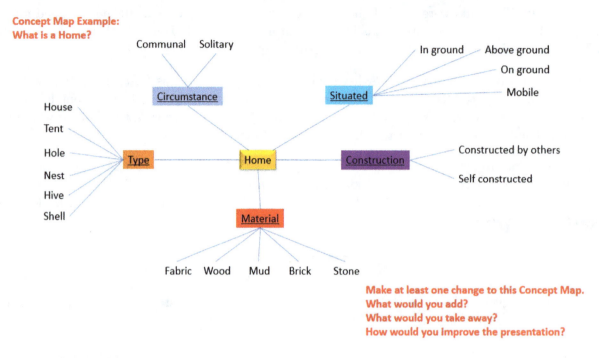

Figure 1.1:

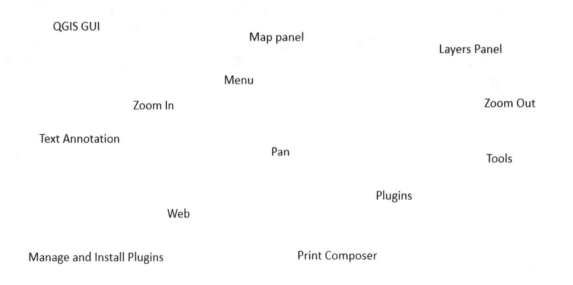

Figure 1.2:

2. Come to My Party

Come to my party - Make your own party invitation

It was cold. I was cold, but certainly not cold enough to wear the coat mother bought for me. Only the really little kids wore coats to school. It was not cool to wear a coat, no matter how cold it was or how stiff my hands became—not to mention my frozen nose and the shivers that ran up my arms under my jumper. I pulled my hands into my sleeves. That was allowed. I nearly stopped walking when I thought about it. Allowed by whom? Hmmm. Something to think about.

At least my stomach was warm. My Mum was almost finished studying at the school for Chefs. At my house, we were eating a lot of very strange foods from all over the world. I had no idea how to pronounce most of it, or even where in the world the ingredients came from. I had to admit though, it all tasted pretty good and though breakfast was nothing like I was accustomed to before she started Chef school, it was incredible. When she finished next month she had a new job lined up with a fancy restaurant in town. Right now she was always looking for ways to practice cooking and for people who wanted to eat.

I hurried up, no dawdling I told myself. I walked as fast as I could to keep warm. The trees arched over the road leading to school. Bare branches hung overhead, the fallen leaves on the ground below. I scuffed my feet through the damp leaves and shivered a bit more. It would be better when the sun was up, if it broke through the clouds. Meanwhile I walked even faster to keep warm, stopping just short of race walking. My PE teacher would have been proud at my speed.

Up ahead I saw a bright pink coat. Who was that? I narrowed my eyes to see if I could glimpse far enough to guess at who would be wearing a padded, winter coat to school. Then I remembered the new girl. I didn't know where she was from, but she had a strange accent even though she spoke English perfectly. She also had a tight look on her face, as though she was afraid. Rightly so, I thought—I would be afraid too if I were new to the school. There were some piranhas in my class. That's what we called the girls who packed together and enjoyed tormenting people not part of their select clique. I had run afoul of them before and knew how sharp they could be when they attacked—and I knew that showing any sign of weakness was a sure way to get attacked. I felt sorry for her. She would learn, but would have to learn the hard way, no doubt. Hmmm. I returned to my earlier thought. Coat wearing was not allowable, was that because of the piranhas? Could be. They certainly loved to make fun of people and were always looking for an opportunity, for a victim.

When I got to the school yard, I slipped through the gate without touching it, careful not to call undue attention to myself. I eased over to the far corner towards my friend who raised a silent hand in greeting.

"Hey," she said. "Another cold day, another school day, another day closer to the weekend."

"Too true," I answered.

"Doing anything this weekend?" she asked, without any real curiosity.

I hesitated for a minute. She was expecting me to say, *No, nothing* as usual, but I suddenly thought maybe

I could—maybe I could do something. In fact, I had a flash of a plan. Maybe *we* could do something. I started to answer, but the bell rang and everyone turned liked well-ordered machinery and started for the school doors.

We dropped our bags beside our desks and waited for the teacher to give us instructions. I noticed the new girl took off her coat and put it over the back of her chair. Some of the other girls giggled behind their hands, watching her when the coat slid to the floor and she had to replace it. She looked around in case there was a better place to hang it, but didn't see one. There were no coat hooks anywhere. You had to get a locker for that, and few of us bothered. Since no one bothered, most of the lockers had been removed. In fact, I had to think about it to remember. Weren't there a few lockers in one of the lower halls, the halls where no one wanted to go because they looked old and abandoned?

Our first class was PE. We marched along the hall to the change room and slipped into our uniforms, tying our shoes as quickly as we could to get into the sports hall before the teacher arrived. She didn't approve of students who were slow. Fast running, fast playing, fast changing. *Fast* was her motto it seemed. First activity for this week was volleyball. I lined up in the center of our court with my friend. The new girl was in front of me. I turned to my friend and pointed with my chin at the new girl.

"I was thinking about having a party," I whispered to her. "Inviting the new girl so that she could meet some people."

"Really," my friend answered softly, out of the side of her mouth, keeping her eye on the ball, apparently surprised at the idea. I had never had a party at my house, not even a birthday party so it was legitimate that she would be surprised, shocked even. "Who would you invite? What would we do?"

I started thinking. Sometimes when I was thinking about something, I lost track of what was happening around me. This was one of those times. The game had started around me and the ball was flying. I heard a shout from the girl who was in the row behind me and I turned around to see what she wanted. Her mouth made a perfect "O" as she watched the ball's trajectory. Smack. The ball hit me square in the behind with a terrific noise. I was so shocked that it unbalanced me and I fell flat on my face. I didn't know what hurt more—my behind, my face, or my feelings.

As my tears fell to the wooden floor, I saw a blurry pair of shoes. My friend was there, squatting down next to where I was laying flat on the floor, my cheek pressed to the wood. She grabbed my arm and propelled me to the edge of the room, past the teacher who nodded silent approval, and through the door that eased shut behind us, closing off the sudden, shrill laughter as the other girls enjoyed the show.

My friend took me to the change room.

"What were you doing—what were you thinking?"

"About the party. How utterly embarrassing," I moaned. "How will I ever live this down. The piranhas will never let me forget this."

"Forget about them. Tell me more about the party idea", she said, trying to distract me from my misery.

"So far, it's just an idea," I said, willing to try to forget what just happened. "I'll tell give you details later when I have it more developed."

Classes went on, the day unfolded more slowly than I could have imagined, with more giggling and finger pointing at me than even the thickest of skins could endure. Still, I had something to think about that took me outside of myself. The party. Who would I invite? What would we do? My friend was right. There were plans to be made. Who cared if the piranhas were having fun at my expense?

That evening I had a discussion with my Mum and she was willing to listen. She was even enthusiastic about it when I described how she could help, and sympathetic when I told her why I thought a party was a good idea. Things were looking up.

Next day I went to the usual corner of the school yard and started to talk to my friend about it.

"The party would be at my house, this Saturday night. My Mum said..."

I didn't get a chance to finish telling her what my Mum said because I heard the loudest member of the piranhas behind me, practically shouting loud enough for the whole school yard to hear.

"A party. At your house, who would come to that?"

I heard hoots of laughter from a few of the other girls, ready to join in trying to embarrass me yet again.

I have to admit my face turned pink, much as I would like to be able to say I kept my cool, but I was scared, nervous, embarrassed, and worried all at the same time. The emotions flooded through me, but I was not going to be silenced. Not this time. What can I lose, I thought? I decided to take a chance.

"Everyone can come," I smiled at her, answering in a loud voice. "It's a *Bring Your Own Invitation* party. Show up at 7 p.m., with an invitation, and you are invited. My Mum is going to cook some of the fanciest recipes from her cooking school and we can all try them out. It will be fun," I said, encouraged by the group gathering around me. "You'll get to try some new kinds of food, special things like what they serve in expensive restaurants, not just pizza and crisps."

"What do you mean, bring our own invitations?" asked a quiet girl from my class.

"That's another idea I had," I answered. "Bring a postcard about yourself, where you come from maybe, or where your parents come from. Share it with everyone else." I looked deliberately at the new girl, smiling widely at her to make sure she knew I was aiming my invitation at her. She nodded, slowly, and I saw a small smile hover at the corner of her mouth.

"What if we don't come from anywhere but here?" one girl asked. "You could get a lot of postcards that are just the same."

"It doesn't have to be where you, personally were born," I repeated. "It could be about anyone in your family or even where you want to go in the future, the place that you think is special for you or your family."

I had their attention now. And so I went right on explaining how they could make a postcard in the mapping program we had in the technology room—the one they could load onto their computers at home for free.

When we got to technology class, I asked the teacher if we could work with QGIS to make invitations for the party. I explained my idea and the teacher was really enthusiastic. She asked me to talk to the class and offered to help as they worked.

QGIS was already loaded on the PCs and there were PDF help files available on the desktop, as well as the online help. I pointed that out to the class. On the screen, I showed them the invitation I made, pointing out things I thought they might want to add, such as labels, shapes, a scale bar and an image (Figure 2.1).

Figure 2.1:

First, I told them, they would need to get a map using the *Menu item: Plugins: Manage and Install Plugins*. Here they would find, in the long alphabetical list of choices, one called *Open Layers Plugin*. Click on *Install*. When they installed that, it would appear in the *Web Menu item* and they could pick from a list of mapped layers from free, online sources. Each of the sources would have choices as well, so they could pick streets or satellite imagery, for example.

Once they selected the source and kind of map, it would appear in the *Layers List* and they would want to zoom to the area of interest using the *Magnifying Glass Tool*, with the plus sign on it, from the tool bar. I pointed out they might also want to use the *Hand Tool* which would allow them to pan around the map. Practicing with all of the tools would allow them to get to just the right scale for the map they wanted to show. I pointed out my map again, saying that I could have done just my neighbourhood, my house and street, but I chose more of what I considered was the area I belonged to—the area I traveled around in with my family while visiting extended family and friends (Figure 2.2, on the next page).

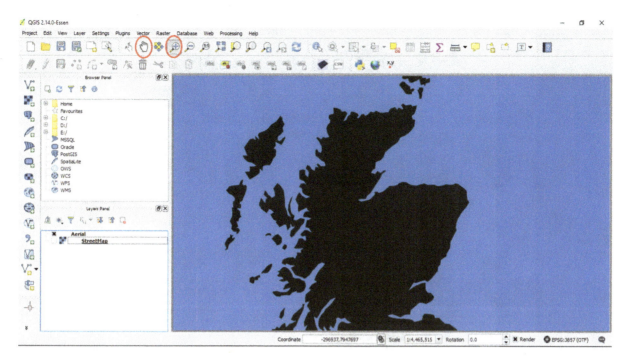

Figure 2.2:

Saving your project is a good idea in case of disaster. *Project Menu: Save*. Give your project a name.

> You want to come to the party? Make your invitation, following along with the instructions.

Now for the map creation.

What is on the map display will show in the *Project Menu: New Print Composer*. The new composer asks for a name, I called it *My Party Invitation*. Then I needed to get the map into the composer from the menu item *Layout: Add Map*.

I clicked in the composer and used a square marquee to draw a square inside the page. The map area I used in the Map View showed up. I noticed the scale was a complicated number, in the *Item Properties: Main Properties: Scale Box*, so I changed it to more even number, to 450,000,000 from 4,415,565, but that was just me being picky—maybe you don't care (Figure 2.3, on the following page).

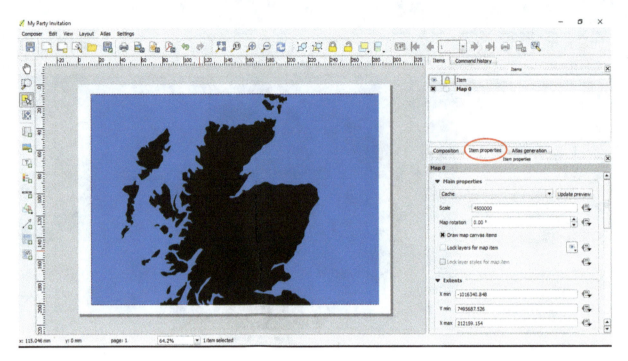

Figure 2.3:

In the *Layout Menu*, I saw a lot of other items and thought they would be good to add to my map: *Scale, Shape, Label, Image*, etc.

I pointed out that I added a border around my map: *Layout/Shape/Rectangle*. In the *Items Panel*, I clicked on *Style: Change*. I clicked on *Fill: Simple Fill*. I made the *Colours: Fill* to be Transparent and the Border to be green. I increased the size of the border to be thicker so it would show up better (Figure 2.4, on the next page).

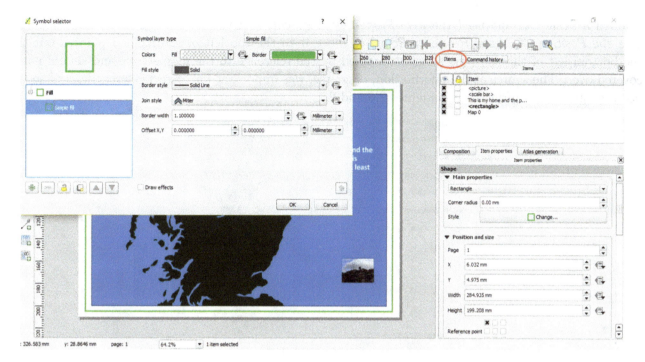

Figure 2.4:

From the *Layout Menu*, I inserted a *Label* that described what I was showing in my invitation. I drew a marquee and typed my message. Then I clicked on *Appearance: Font* and made it bold, changed the colour, and increased the font size (Figure 2.5).

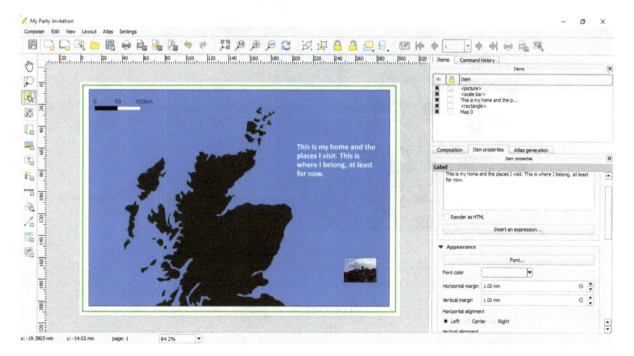

Figure 2.5:

I added a Scale Bar and used the *Item Properties: Segments* (set to 0 left and 2 right) and *Properties: Size and Position (X, Y and Reference Point)* to move it to the top left of the map. I pointed out that the bottom left of the map was already occupied by the reference to the map source and should not be covered over. The source of the information, of course, was important for correct referencing and so that no copyrights were infringed. See Figures 2.6 and 2.7.

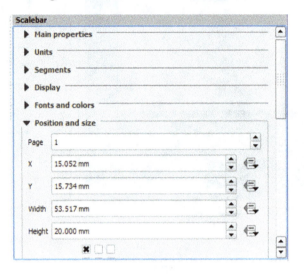

Figure 2.6:

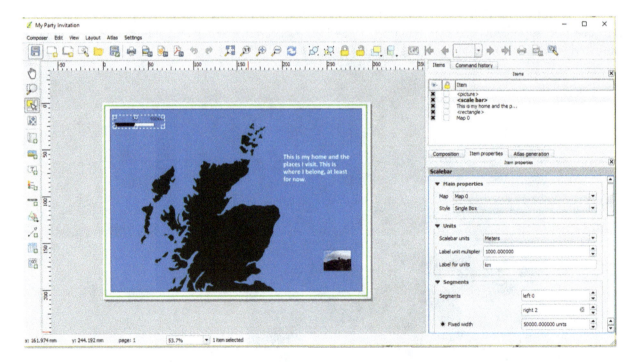

Figure 2.7:

If you want to explore in more detail, you might want to look at the following in the QGIS manuals:

Training Manual

- Module: The Interface- Lesson: An Overview of the Interface

- Module: Creating Maps- Lesson: Using Map Composer

QGIS User Guide

- General Tools/Zooming and Panning

- Print Composer

I looked up at the class. Lots of people were nodding. Some were talking to each other, pointing at my map and discussing what they might do. I hoped it was going to be a success.

_____

The next morning, after the party, I woke up and went through a check list in my mind.

The new girl that started school with a tight face left the party with a happy smile and a lot of new friendships to explore. *Check.*

The new girl had brought a tray of food that my mother leapt upon, intrigued with the exotic selection. When I went to the kitchen for extra servings partway through the party, I heard my mother on the phone to her mother asking questions about ingredients. I had liked the food; my mother was sure to use the new recipes and was thrilled to have made a new friend with extraordinary recipes to share. *Check.*

Most of my class had come to the party, but only one piranha put in an appearance. Without the rest of her "school" patrolling on the offensive, she was actually quite friendly and fun to be with. *Check,* with a question mark. This was something needing further thought to figure out. A school of piranhas was dangerous, a solitary one was not. Why? Hmmm.

Everyone brought a party invitation and was proud to show them off. I collected them and was going to make a book to give to the new girl. Some of them were really good. Some of my class were good at working with the mapping program and some were just really artistic. I was going to have a good look at all of the maps as I compiled the book so I could learn something from everyone else. *Check.*

All-in-all, a very good party.

> Now you make your invitation. Add the words in *bold, italic* to your Concept Map. Could you plan a party like this one?

3. Freedom

I was panting. I could hardly breathe. I had never run so fast. Above me the tree branches were whipping around on the grey sky. A few breaks in the dark clouds showed morning was on its way, but that it would be a wet, grey day. I wondered how much of it I would be able to have. I thought my end might be near.

As I raced up the hill, the noise of the wind in the trees and the bushes along the side of the road momentarily masked the noise of my pursuer. I was glad I could no longer hear the harsh breath or the noise of my tracker's racing pace on the road, following me relentlessly since it made my fear unbearable. But it also meant I no longer knew how close he or she was and that was a danger as well. Any moment might be my last. I didn't slow down. I ran and ran. I knew I had been seen and that my straight route along the road made me an easy quarry. I needed to get off of the road. Fast.

There, I marked, a break in the bushes under the black trunk of a tree. It looked as if, if I could just get there before being caught, I might find some safety. Where I found the last reserves to leap for the gap, I'll never know, but I did and threw myself into a hole I spied, at the last moment, between two roots. I hurled myself into the damp tunnel and flattened my body against the mud wall. I shivered, I moaned, I breathed in short, harsh gasps. I was terrified, but was safe, or so I thought.

Just then a black nose shoved through the hole and snuffled around on the floor of the tunnel, only inches from my long back foot. I hastily shifted my legs further down the tunnel, still standing upright, with my back pressed firmly against the wall. In a moment, the nose was replaced with a yellow eye. I stopped breathing and waited in total silence. I could see the eye trying to pick me out of the gloom. My tell-tale tail was tucked. That flash of white was not going to give me away twice, I vowed.

The night was not finishing as it started, that was for sure. At the beginning of the evening, short hours ago, we had a party, my brothers and sisters and I, listening to last words of wisdom from our mother, in between nibbles of delicious sun-warmed flowers and merry chases over and around the tunnel entrances, rolling when we stumbled from running too quickly over the hummocks of grass. I knew I should have paid more attention to those words of wisdom, after all my mother had lived a good few years and had watched over a good few events that occurred in our fields and along the edges of the paths and roads where we sometimes encountered things not conducive to our survival, let alone our good health. She had done her best with us, and with me, but I knew I could have done better, better at listening, especially after she showed me the error of my ways more than once. My tail. With me, it was always my tail.

When I was still so young that I could barely move without help, I heard one of my family say, "My, what a beautiful tail that young one has. Magnificent. Look at the size. Look at the colour."

"Yes," agreed my mother, proud of the compliment, but becoming thoughtful as she considered the implications. "It is beautiful, but a tail like that can get a rabbit into trouble. Tails are there to help us escape, but if they flash too brightly, they can attract too much attention as well."

As I grew, more comments came about my lovely tail and I reveled in them. Soon I was carrying my tail as high as I could, to show it off. It was lovely. Even in the reflection from puddles I could see how magnificent it looked, arched up over my back. That night, after a nuzzle goodbye from my family, I hopped off, tail straight up. Proud as ever.

Now, covered in dirt from the tunnel wall, quivering with fear, my tail was not nearly so much loved by me. It very nearly cost me my life. When it flashed in the lights of a passing car, I saw two orange eyes mark my location and begin to head towards me at full speed. Now I was the incipient meal and my celebratory place at the going-away party was over. I was so lucky to find the tunnel just in time. I looked at the entrance, getting ready to heave a sigh of relief. The eye had retreated at last, but I couldn't quite believe I was out of the woods, as yet, so to speak. I brushed a root off of my ear and waited, quietly.

First it was the nose, then the eye, now the paws. Two slim, white paws began to dig into the tunnel entrance, scrabbling in the loose dirt, making the entrance wider. That fox was determined. It must have been really hungry, or must have found the look of my plump body and beautiful tail to be entirely too appetizing, too enticing to pass up. I was going to have to get out of there and fast.

Abandoning silence and the camouflage offered to my brown fur by the side of the tunnel, I loped off on the downward trajectory, hoping the tunnel would be a long one, with rocks that would hamper the excavation occurring at the entrance. More than anything else, I hoped the tunnel would lead to a safe place and escape. Onward I ran.

Soon the tunnel walls closed in on me. No light. I let my whiskers touch the tunnel walls in an exploratory way, feeling for any potential side passages. Nothing. Only straight on. At least the noise of the digging behind me was gone. It was too far back now, even for my sharp ears.

Just when I thought all might be lost and I was going to have to wait it out, hoping the fox would grow tired and leave, I saw a gleam of light ahead. It was too bright for the sun at this time of morning. I hesitated. There was an opening, shaped by a triangle of wood nailed together, and beyond that, more light. Cautiously I hopped forward and poked my nose through to investigate.

It was like a huge nest, a square nest. Not made by digging, but shaped by people I guessed, who built it with wood from trees. It smelled of people, but I didn't see anyone. Should I risk going in? What would I find?

Now for your part. You are going to *digitize* (digitally draw) *Vector Layers*.

You have found out that a map is being commissioned by the rabbit, after the incredible escape from the room at the end of the tunnel. The rabbit wants to use the map to tell others about the adventure and the route. You think you can do the job and decide to create part of the information needed, just to show the rabbit what you can do and see if you will be hired to do all the work. A map for a rabbit is not quite the same as a map you would make for humans. You may wish to follow the illustrations and instructions below, at least for a start, but deviate from them to create work that you think the rabbit would prefer.

At a minimum, the rabbit wants you to:

- Draw the opening to the tunnel.

- Draw the triangle that led to the room.

- Draw the room.

- Draw the escape.

How did the rabbit escape from the room? The good news is the rabbit survived to tell the tale and has told you how the escape occurred and what you will need to draw. Now you tell us using the map. Was it right away, directly from the room, or were there interim steps? You will finish the story with the help of your new, furry, potential employer.

Don't forget—use the instructions below as a starting point, but you don't need to make your work be exactly what is suggested here, and make sure you add the words in *Bold, italic*, or any other software concepts to your Concept Map.

First you will need to use the *Project Menu: New*. *Save* it with a name, perhaps *Freedom*, as in this chapter.

Next you will need to use the *Layer Menu: Create Layer: New Shapefile Layer*. (Figure 3.1)

Figure 3.1:

You will choose *Polygon* from the choices, although you could also choose *Line* or *Point*. Think of how you need to model the world you are going to draw before you make your choices. If you want to draw a river, for instance, you might use one line, or you might use a polygon and give the river width. Modeling the world in a map depends on what you want to show. For now, use polygon and then experiment later with other methods and thoughts.

Type the *Name* of the *New Field*: RoutePart. Click *Add to fields list*. (Figure 3.2)

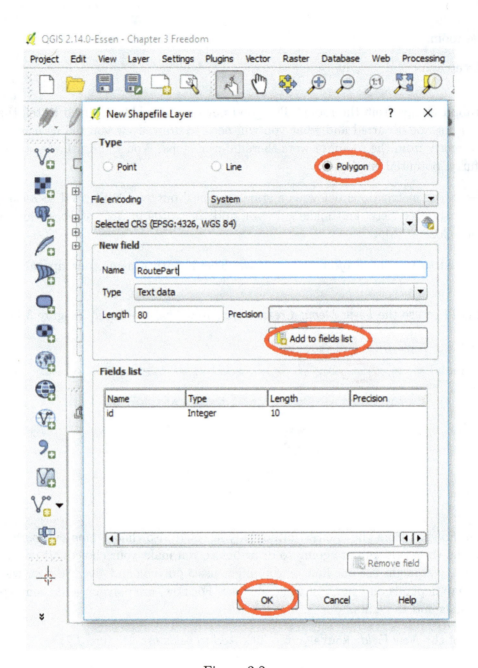

Figure 3.2:

Click *OK*. Save the new shapefile with the *File Name*: `RabbitRouteParts`. It will now show up in your *Layers Panel* with a default fill colour. (Figure 3.3)

Figure 3.3:

You will want to change the default rendering of the shapefile so it looks more like what the rabbit has described to you: a hole, a tunnel, an opening, and a room.

Double click on the colour square beside the Layer name, or right click on the Layer name and select *Properties*. Both methods will bring up the *Layer Properties* so that you can work with the colours and fill.

Click on Style and the *Simple Fill* to bring up the *Symbol Layer Type* dialogue. Click on the *Fill* and choose Transparent. Click on the *Border* and choose the colour black. Click on the *Border Width* and increase it to a larger number so that you have a thick border that will show up well. Click on OK when you are finished. (Figure 3.4)

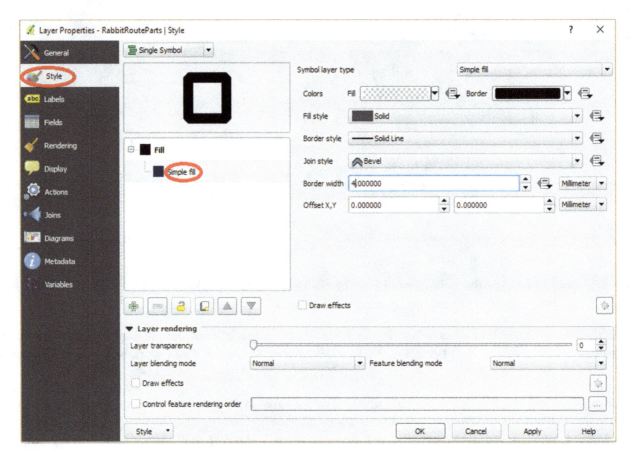

Figure 3.4:

Now you want to add the first shape. Click on the *Pencil Tool*.

Click on the icon that allows you to add a *Circular String*. Draw something that is basically circular. Right click on the line to end the circle. Don't forget this part. Always right click to end when you are finished drawing. A dialogue box will pop up and allow you to add an ID Number. This is the first part, so type in 1. Then add the name of the RoutePart. Type in `Hole`. (Figure 3.5)

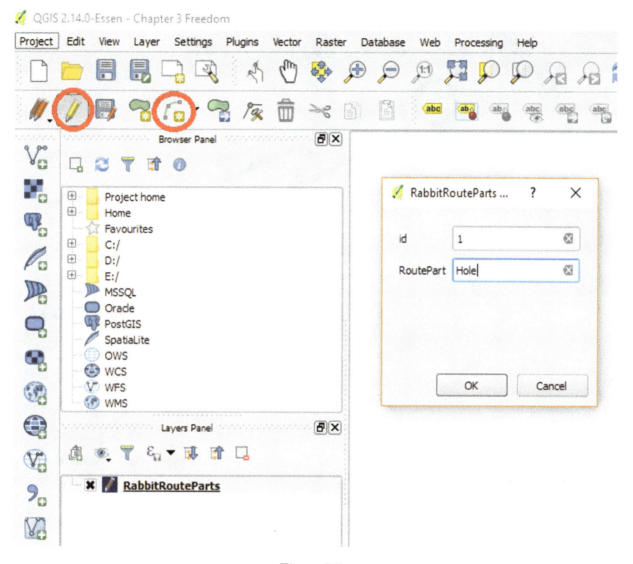

Figure 3.5:

Click on the *Pencil Tool* again to stop editing and to save your edits.

Click on the *Pencil Tool*. Add the tunnel with the **Add Feature Tool**. You can find it between the Pencil Tool and the Circular String tool. Add the ID Number (2) and the RoutePart name (Tunnel).

Repeat for the Opening and the Room.

For additional help, you might want to check out:

- *QGIS User Guide/Working with Vector Data/Editing*

- *QGIS Training Manual/Module: Creating Vector Data/Lesson: Creating a New Vector Dataset*

Your map might look something like Figure 3.6.

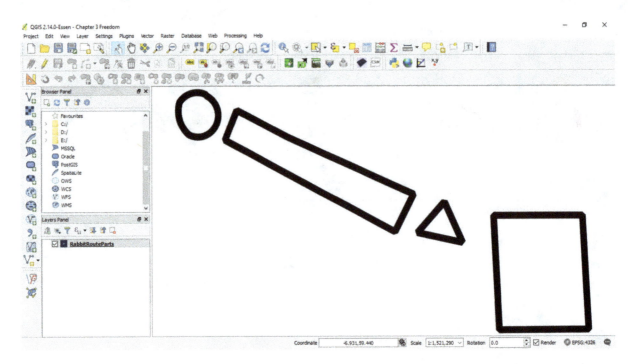

Figure 3.6:

Click on the *Pencil* icon again to stop editing. Save your edits one more time. It is always a good idea to save frequently.

Now right click on the RabbitRouteParts layer in the *Layers Panel* and choose to *Open the Attribute Table*. Click on one of the rows. Notice that the selected row highlights the shape in your map. The table draws what is in the map. The table is the most important part of your mapping work. The map is only a way to visualise your table. That is something you might want to remember and think about when you use any GIS software. (Figure 3.7)

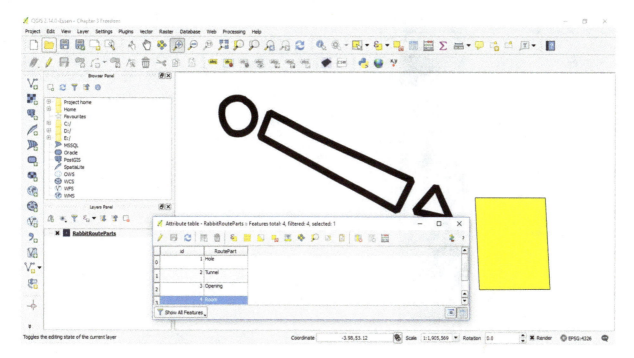

Figure 3.7:

To unselect the shape, use *View: Select/Deselect Features from All Layers*.

Now comes the part that only you know about. How does the rabbit get out of the room? To draw more on your map canvas, use the *Zoom Out Tool* (Magnifying Glass with the Subtract Sign on it). You may also want to use the Pan Hand Tool to move the map to a different location so that you can have the space you need to add features to the table and the map.

After you have finished, add *Labels* to the map, using what you typed into the table. Right click on the Layer. Choose *Properties*. Choose *Labels*. You will need to select: *Show Labels for this Layer*. You will want to change the colour and the font but there are a lot of other things you could experiment with as well. (Figures 3.7 and 3.8)

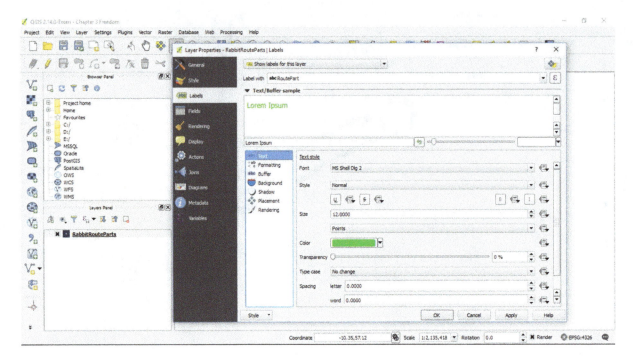

Figure 3.8:

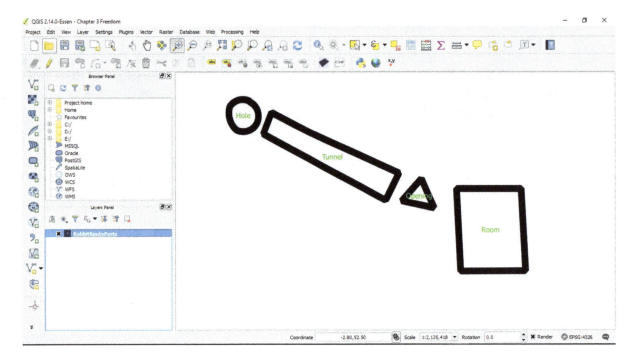

Figure 3.9:

Will the rabbit like it? Do you want to add anything else to make sure you get the job? I hope the rabbit doesn't get carried away telling others about the adventure and forget what was learned from the troubles caused by too much pride in a tail. What do you think?

4. Treasure Hunt

I live in a small town, really small. Having nothing to do is a frequent complaint of people my age. You can watch TV and movies, watch TV and movies with friends, play computer games, or play computer games with friends. Or you can sit in the park at the picnic tables no one uses for picnics and talk with your friends. When it is school holiday times and your friends are gone, choices for something to do are cut in half: watch TV or movies, play computer games, or sit at the picnic table and stare into the distance. Not very appealing. Luckily my town, although small, still has a public library and it's open every day. Not a place to go with friends since laughing and talking are frowned on by the librarian, but a place to go when you are alone. My Mum works and we don't go on holidays very often.

So, here I am, sitting at a table in the public library with a stack of books in front of me. I could search for books that I know of and would be interested in reading, but I can do that anytime. When I come to sit in the library, planning to stay for the afternoon, with rain streaking the window behind me, I prefer to take books from random shelves and see what I can find. Sort of like a treasure hunt. I pretend that the books are calling to me and it isn't chance or coincidence I select them and pull them into the pile growing in my arms, but that it is fate causing me to select them. A fate that will be revealed when I start looking through them. The rules are: any book can be selected, but I am not allowed to read the title or author until I am sitting at the table.

Back at the table I ease the pile from my arms to the table, being careful not to make any loud noises as I lower them onto the wooden surface of the table. I sit on the chair and adjust it to bring me closer to the table. The scraping noise of the chair legs earns me a sharp look from the librarian and I let the hair fall over my face to hide from the accusatory glare.

First book. Nice cover, green leather, smells old, as if it hasn't been read for fifty years, if ever. I open it up to thumb through the pages but it is bigger than I think and the cover knocks against my carefully placed stack of volumes. Over it goes, bang, bang, bang, each book hitting the floor with a clap like thunder. Now the librarian is not just glaring, the librarian's eyes are flaming. Quickly I bend under the table to pick up the books and place them soundlessly on the table. One book is really far under the table and I have to crawl to get it. By the time I can reach it, the library is hushed once again. I fumble my way back into my seat without causing another sound and look at the book in my hand.

A book about 19th century poetry. I don't mind poetry. I rifled through the book and stopped at a page with writing on it. Nearly illegible. Whoever wrote it had messier handwriting than me and that was something I thought would be hard to do. Then I looked at the first page of the book, where the previous owner wrote his name, and saw it belonged to Gordon W. Simpson. I looked again, surprised. Gordon Simpson was my neighbour. When I was little I used to take cakes my mother baked to him. He is alone in the world, said my mother, and he needs to know that someone cares. Mr. Simpson was always kind to me and thanked me for the cakes as though I had baked them myself. He was old when I was seven, now he was ANCIENT. He couldn't even walk anymore. Now he used a chair and had a person come by to visit each day to give him special care. Once though, he had been part of the world and he had been a university professor, dashing off to the university and all over the world, according to what my mother had told me.

I decided to check the book out and to try to decipher the notes on the page. I was curious about what Mr. Simpson had written. I put the book under my coat to protect it from the rain and walked home through the gloomy streets.

Next day, after spending quite some time working with the book, I showed it to my mother and she laughed at Mr. Simpson's writing.

"The only person who could translate that is the writer," she said. "Why don't you take it over to him? You can take him this tin of cake at the same time."

I thought it was a good idea and knocked on the door, only to be answered by the caregiver. She took the tin and thanked me, but told me Mr. Simpson was resting.

"Who's there?" shouted a voice as she started to shut the door.

"It's the child from next door," she answered.

"I always want my visitors to be welcome," he said, overruling her.

Smiling and shrugging, she opened the door to me and bade me come in. I went through to the library and greeted Mr. Simpson who smiled happily to see me.

"It's been so long," he said. "So lovely to see you again. I'll bet you've brought something along with you. Mrs. Inglewood, could you serve us some of the lovely baking that my neighbour has kindly delivered, for us all to share?"

Sitting in the book-lined library with a piece of cake and tea in front of us, I brought the book out of my bag and handed it to Mr. Simpson.

"Ah!" he smiled happily. "Cake and a surprise. Wonderful. And it gets better, as you will see." He opened the book and leafed through it until he found the annotated page. "Did you read this?"

I admitted I tried but that the message eluded me.

"Quite right," he said, "I meant it to be cryptic. It is the first clue for a treasure hunt." His voice became very soft and I leaned in to hear more clearly, "Do you want to give it a try?" he asked. "Sailors have not been using latitude and longitude for very long, relatively, to record their location, but once they started, the degrees, minutes and seconds, in both latitude and longitude they used are like exact addresses for every location on earth," he explained. "What I found, on a scrap of map in an old library were some locations and a few words that gave me the idea something of value has been buried on the beach very near here. There are coordinates to show where a ship was anchored, where some people made landfall, and then a list of distances and directions followed before the burial of the 'items' took place."

"Do you know what it was? Didn't you try to find it?" I asked.

He smiled and shook his head. "By the time I found this paper," he said regretfully, "I was too old to go off on a treasure hunt." He showed me the geographic coordinates and then copied over the text that he had found detailing the next steps and handed it to me. "Make the map", he told me. "Find the treasure!"

———————————————

> What is the treasure? Where is it? Follow along, help me make the route and let's see what we find.

Mr. Simpson's instructions started with a set of coordinates. X and Y. I had to get to that place. Since X and Y and the numbers associated with them didn't match any street address or description of my area, I knew I would first have to figure out what my X, Y was and then move to the X, Y where I needed to be. His writing, even though he had taken care, still wasn't that easy to read, but I gave it a try.

I took out a paper map we had at home. I noticed the paper map had markings around the outside, a grid of coordinates.

My location was -227229, 7835647. The latitude and longitude I needed to get to was Latitude 57.319, Longitude -1.979.

The map had a note that said it was using UTM coordinates for the grid. I had to start somewhere and, the Internet was a good place to start. I typed Latitude and Longitude to UTM into the Search on a browser and found that there was a calculator for the conversion. According to the conversion, the X, Y I needed to get to was -220260, 7825569. Let's find out if I can ride my bike to the place from which the people began their walk along the shore. We need to draw in the route.

I don't know much about maps, but I know there is a difference between a map and a globe. Flat maps use projections. They take the round world and stretch it around so it can be drawn on a flat screen or on a piece of paper. When the world is round, the units are geographic units, latitude and longitude, not projected units. Since we are using a piece of paper and a screen to map, we want to work with projections and projected units. How the world is referenced, whether with geographic or projected units is called a *Coordinate Reference System* (CRS).

Read more about CRS and how it works in the *QGIS Training Manual: Module: Vector Analysis, Lesson: Reprojecting and Transforming Data.*

To make the map, first you will need to use the *Project Menu: New*. *Save* it with a name, perhaps `Treasure`.

Go to *Settings Menu: Options/CRS*, click in the radio button, *Automatically enable on the fly reprojection*. We don't want to have different kinds of units in our map or else things won't line up. From *Always start new projects with the following CRS*, click on the Globe icon and select the one with */Pseudo Mercator, EPSG:3857*. We want to use projected coordinates, a flat map, not geographic coordinates from GPS and a globe.

Use the *Web* Menu Item and select a *Street Map*. You will draw the route on the map, tracing a street, so we have a record of the route while I ride there on my bike. But first, create the start and end points for my journey.

Go to *Layer: Create Layer: New Shapefile* and add a new layer, selecting *Type: Point, New Field: Name*, `Location` (*Type: Text data, Length* 10, *Add to fields list*) and save it with the name `StartAndEnd`. To start at my location, you will need to find it. Go to *Plugins: Manage and Install Plugins*. Install the *Zoom to Coordinates Tool*. Using *X,Y, Zoom to Coordinates Tool*, type in my starting location (Figure 4.1, on the next page).

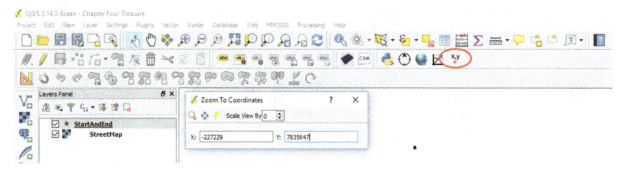

Figure 4.1:

Use the *Flash Point Icon* on the tool to direct you and zoom into my starting point. Make StartAndEnd the *Active Layer* by clicking on it. Use the *Pencil Tool* to start editing the StartAndEnd layer. Put a point where you will start the route as shown by the *X,Y Tool*. Give it the ID number 1 and the Name, Start. Now find the place where we want to be, using the X,Y Tool and the coordinates given above. Use the Pan To Icon on the tool and put a point with the ID number 2 and the Name, End (Figure 4.2).

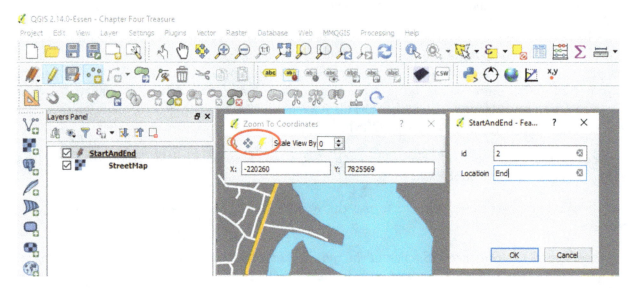

Figure 4.2:

To see the whole route, right click on the StartAndEnd layer and select *Zoom to Layer*.

Now create the route of the journey. Go to *Layer: Create Layer: New Shapefile* and add a new layer, selecting *Line*. Use the *Pencil Tool* to toggle editing, add a new feature clicking along the route you think I should travel. Right click to end. *Save* your work and call it Route. You will probably want to change the symbol for the route. Double click on the layer in the layer list. Select *Style: Width* and *Colour*. Now use the Measure Tool to measure the length of the route by clicking along it. What do you think? Could I ride my bicycle, or do I need a bus? See Figure 4.3, on the next page.

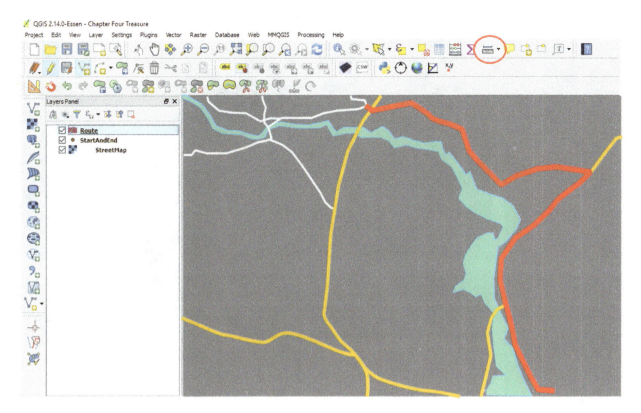

Figure 4.3:

For walking along the beach, roads will no longer be helpful. Add a *Satellite or Aerial Map* from the *Web Menu: Open Layers Plugin*. The new map will draw over the top of the route. Drag and drop it below the two shapefiles you created so they draw over the top of the aerial view (Figure 4.4, on the following page).

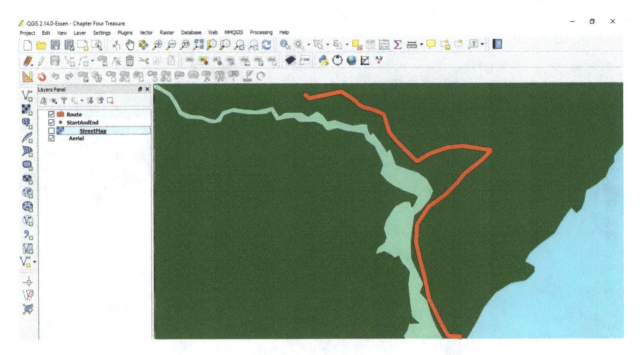

Figure 4.4:

The instructions say that the people who buried the treasure walked certain distances and directions, specifically:

- 1 mile (5280 feet - distance) at 20 degrees (azimuth)

- 0.5 mile (2640 feet - distance) at 50 degrees (azimuth)

- 1000 feet (distance) at 130 degrees (azimuth)

These directions are given from the degrees on a compass. Think of a compass as being a circle. Circles have 360 degrees. Both 0 and 360 are at the top, the north. East is 90, the south 180 and the west 270 degrees. So 20 degrees is towards the northeast, as is 50 degrees, while 130 degrees is between east and south.

You will need to load a plugin to map the distance and direction. Click on *Plugins: Manage and Install Plugins: Azimuth and Distance Plugin* and *Install*. Find and use the plugin from *Plugins: Topography: Azimuth and Distance*.

The Active layer should be the Route line that you made. Click on it to highlight it.

We don't really need to keep the line to find the treasure, but if we are going to add a line, we need a line shapefile to add it to. It won't work to add a line to a point or a polygon shapefile. Click on *Options: Feet*. Click on *Drawing: Starting Point: From Map* and click on the point you created on the map, that is, click where the route line ends. Click *Close* on that popup. Now add the values for the route in the Azimuth and Distance fields, as specified above (20, 5280/50, 2650/130, 1000). After the addition of each pair of numbers, click *Add to Bottom*. After each addition, use the *Pan Hand* icon to pan the map to the next point. See Figure 4.5, on the next page and Figure 4.6, on page 54.

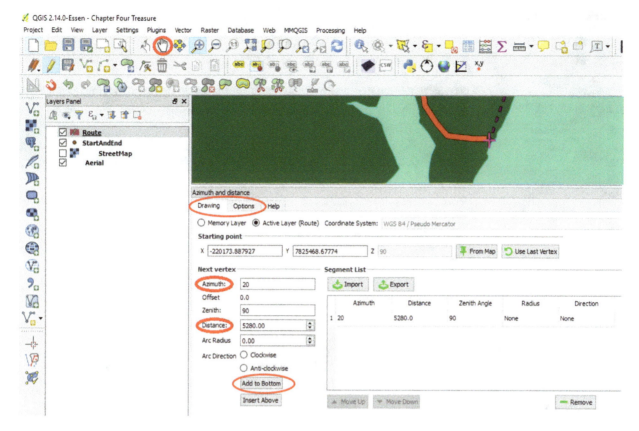

Figure 4.5:

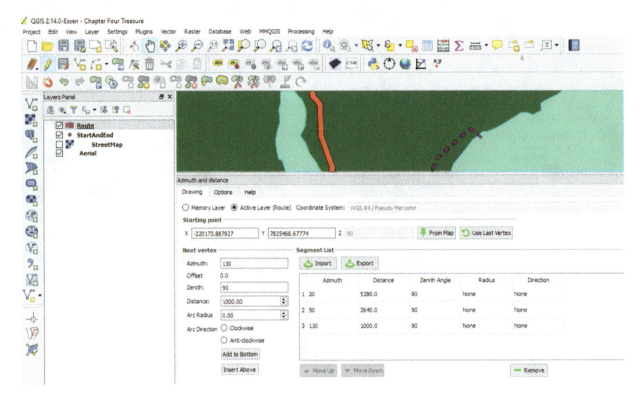

Figure 4.6:

Now click on the StartAndEnd layer and click on the *Pencil Tool* to change the editing layer to the points layer. Click on *Add a Feature*. Put a point right where the end of the new line is. That is where we have to go. Name it `Treasure Site`. *Save* your edits to the points shapefile.

Okay, now we have the map. You might want to print it out. It looks like a very interesting area to explore. I can't wait to show Mr. Simpson and then plan our next steps. Where do you think the treasure could be found? Any ideas?

5. Just Give it a Try

I mashed my hands against my ears. I screwed my eyes shut so tightly I could see bright lights behind my eyelids. I did not want to hear the announcement. I did not want to have my heart broken. The muted roar I could hear from the microphone ceased, all was quiet. Cautiously I opened my eyes and took down my hands. What had happened?

It started a month ago as I was walking down the hall at school. A group was standing around a poster on the wall beside the technology room. Their backs and shoulders were tight against each other, craning to see and read the poster. They were talking excitedly among themselves. I slid by into the room, intending to look at the poster once they were gone. It was not acceptable for a person like me to interfere and grab a spot when the cool kids were busy with something. They would have shouldered me aside at best, or at worst, stared at me with cold, disbelieving eyes. I didn't know which felt worse, directly being pushed out of the way, or being made to feel worthless. Negative physical or emotional reactions; neither one was top of my list for being conducive to happiness. I tried to avoid confrontation when I could. Think small, stay quiet. It was a policy that had stood me in good stead up until now.

It turned out that I did not have to wait until the class was over to find out what was on the poster. The teacher announced it right at the start.

"You will likely have read the poster outside the door, but for those of you who were too late," he looked pointedly at a few of the students who were perpetually the last through the door, "I'll fill you in. There is a fantastic opportunity for one of you, one very hard working and lucky student, to travel to a technology fair during the school break. All costs, travel, accommodation, food, and even entry to some extra events, will be covered by the scholarship."

We were all listening intently. Hands shot up to ask questions.

"Yes," the teacher pointed to one of the kids who had been blocking the poster when I walked into the room.

"Will it be one person from our school, or one person from our district?"

"One from the district," answered the teacher. "You will have competition from your classmates as well as from the other local schools." He pointed to another student.

"Will the judging be based on how technology is used, or on what technology is used, or. . . ?"

"The information on the poster is pretty clear" he answered. "The work has to be based on digital technology, but it states there is quite a lot of room for interpretation on what constitutes an innovative approach to using that technology. There are also no limits on what technology can be used."

There was a buzz of conversation in the class. I was quiet. For me to win would be a dream come true. I liked technology class and I liked working with computers, but I certainly didn't have all of the cool programs at home that most of the other kids had. My Mum worked two jobs and long hours. I didn't have the latest computer games or apps. I didn't even have a mobile device to use when I was outside of school. Winning? Me? It seemed more than unlikely. Still, my Mum always told me that you couldn't get anywhere if you didn't try, so I thought, why not. Maybe there was something I could do, even with my old PC and none of the latest software.

When we left the class, I read the poster very carefully and made notes on what I needed to hand in at the end of the month, a week before school break. I needed a poster and an essay about my poster. I had some investigation to do.

Note to self, I thought: not all software costs. Even the usual software functions can be used innovatively with a little creative thinking. That's it, I thought. Creativity… art… technology as art. Now I knew I was onto something. Maybe it was time I stopped thinking small and being quiet. Maybe I had a chance to do something where my work could speak for me. Maybe…

The QGIS mapping program was on my PC desktop. Maps, I thought? Maps are about information, information delivered with a grid. Rigid information. I started to look around at some other programs but I kept thinking about maps. Maps were about information, but the information was something that could have a message. Not all of the maps I had seen were like the maps in the car, the ones we used to get from one place to another on the road. What if I could make a map that showed more than just roads?

I thought about really old maps I had seen, ones that had parts of the world drawn all wrong, maps with huge empty spaces—or ones that filled in the blank spots with imaginary beings, blowing winds from the corners of the map, maps with the oceans filled with monsters. Those maps were people's ideas about what the world looked like as well as warnings about the world. What if I wanted to make a map that illustrated how I thought about the world? What would I put in it?

> What would you put in it? You might want to read first before you decide. Get some ideas from following along, but be sure to do things in your own way to reflect your own thoughts and feelings. If you create something and then change your mind, you can remove Layers by right clicking on them and selecting Remove.

I opened up the mapping program and added the satellite image from *Web: OpenLayers plugin*. I zoomed into my town with the *Magnifying Glass* tool. I used *Layer: Create Layer* and created a *New Shapefile*, for `Points`. I typed `Place` into *Name* and then clicked *Add to fields list*. I saved the new Shapefile naming it `MyPlaces`. I clicked on the MyPlaces layer in the *Layers Panel* to make it the active layer (Figure 5.1, on the next page)

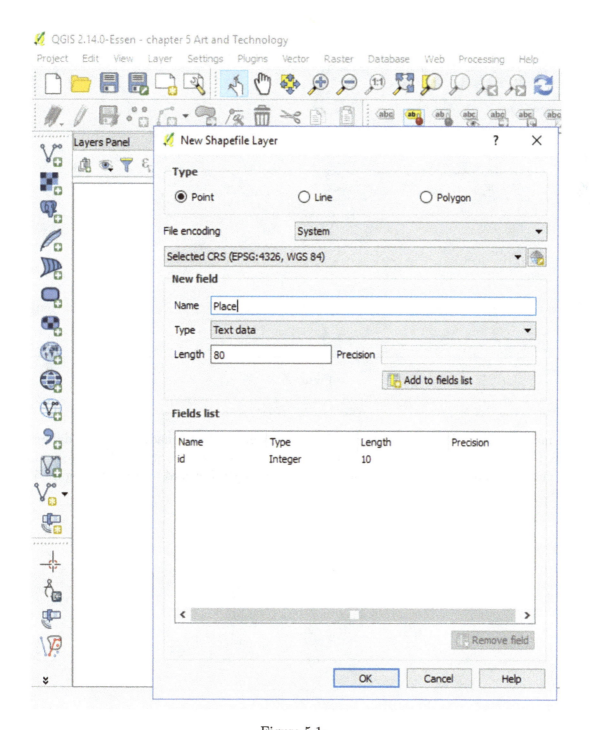

Figure 5.1:

Now I wanted to add points for my house, my school, my grandparents' house, my friends' houses, and the place I went to sometimes when I went for a walk by myself, the place I liked to sit and think. I clicked on the *Pencil* tool, used *Add Feature* tool, and clicked on map to add a point at the correct location. I typed in the ID and the Name and continued to add points until it was done. I clicked on the *Pencil* again and selected *Save*. Then I wanted to add some dots very far away, to show the places I had been to on holidays so I started editing again, with the *Pencil* and *Add Feature* (Figure 5.2, on the following page).

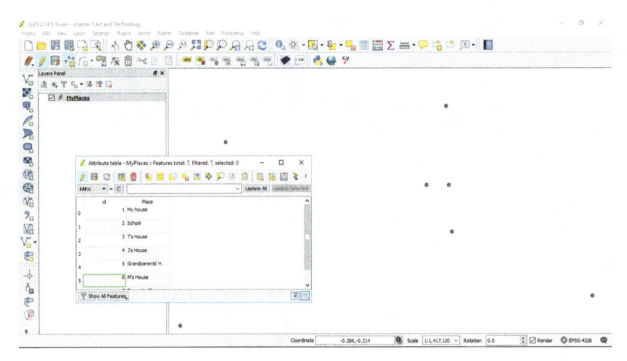

Figure 5.2:

Dots on a map. Hmmm. Not very artistic. I added some colour. First I made each dot a different colour. To do this I right clicked on the *Layer*, MyPlaces. I chose *Properties: Style*. Then, instead of *Single Symbol*, I chose *Categorized*. Under *Column*, I chose *Place*. Then I clicked on *Classify* (Figure 5.3, on the next page).

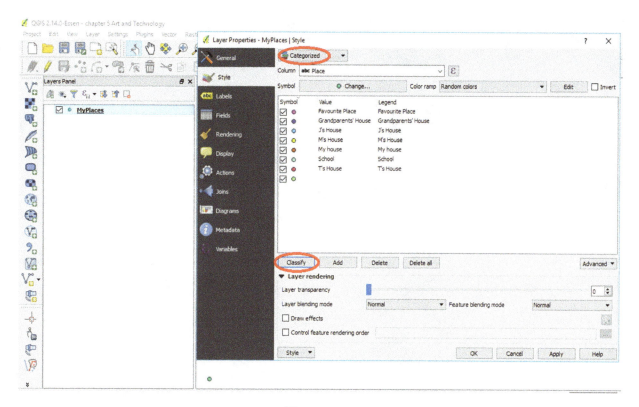

Figure 5.3:

I looked and took off the outline of the dot so that it wouldn't be black.

I changed the size of the dots to make them bigger so that they would stand out more (Figure 5.4, on the following page).

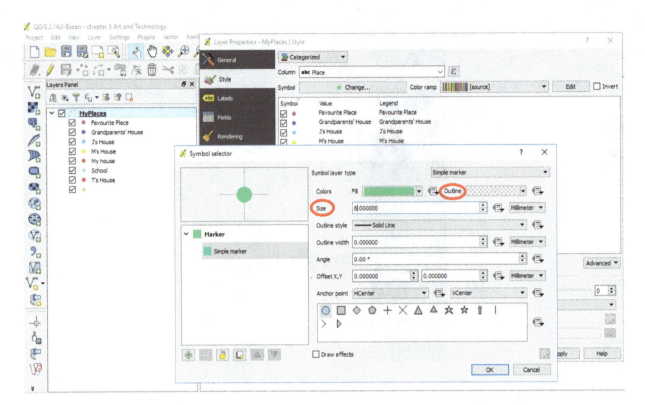

Figure 5.4:

Then I had a really good idea. What if I got rid of the background map and just had the dots. Then it wouldn't just look like dots on a map, it would look like dots, but they were dots with meaning. Now I was getting somewhere. My school, what colour did it represent to me. I made it a mustardy yellow. Not because I thought of it like sunshine, but because I read that yellow is a colour that people find disturbing. I thought of school as a place that made me confused and sad sometimes but sometimes gave me feelings of accomplishment. I wasn't always sure what to think about school. My house, what colour would I make it? Hmmm, not always good, not always bad. I couldn't make all my dots yellow.

I thought for a bit, and came up with a different idea. The places in my life weren't dots, they were more like areas that influenced me. How much influence did they have on me? My home, for example, had more influence on me than my friends' houses. My favourite place had a lot of influence on how I saw the rest of the world. School had influence, but was it as much as home? Zones of influence—buffers.

I had seen maps that showed circles around areas, for example how many people could be served by a store. That helped the chain stores to decide where to put their stores so that they could get the most customers. I had seen other filled in areas around rivers to show how far the water would spill over the banks of the river if there was a flood. I knew, from my reading in the mapping program's help files that these things were called buffers. So far, so good.

I looked at my dots on the map and decided that there were too many. If I wanted to show something, I had better get rid of the outliers. The holidays were great, but if I couldn't zoom in to a certain area, it would be difficult to show all that I wanted to show with any detail. I deleted the holiday dots.

Then I thought about all of my friends. There were a lot of them over the years; some had moved away, some had been best friends for a while, but were not as close now. With some regret, I decided to delete the friends' houses dots. This map was going to be about me, about my regular journeys and the places I went to—how I felt about them.

Without the background map, I could do even more. I could move the dots to show what the distances traveled meant to me. The walk to school was usually really long; sometimes I dragged my feet on the way there, sometimes I was really tired on the way home. The walk to my favourite place was always short. I was always thinking and I would get there before I knew it. My grandparents' house was a long way away, by car, but it was always a happy journey because it was fun going there. My home was at the center of how I felt and who I was. I rearranged the places on the map. Now I was using the map to communicate.

To delete the features, I used the *Pencil Tool* to toggle editing on, then the *Select Tool* to select the point. Then I used the *Delete Selected Tool*. I had to right click on the layer and select *Properties* to *Classify* the points again so the table Layer Panel would update (Figure 5.5).

Figure 5.5:

To move the points to where I wanted them, I made sure I was editing the correct Layer. I clicked on the *Select Tool*, clicked on the *Feature*, clicked on the *Move Features Tool* and then dragged the feature to where I wanted it (Figure 5.6).

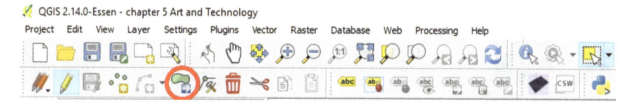

Figure 5.6:

I clicked on the *Pencil* again and saved my edits.

Now it was time for the buffers. To create a buffer, first I read about them in the *QGIS Training Manual: Vector Analysis: 7.2.8.* Then I used the menu item, *Vector/Geoprocessing Tools/Buffer(s)*. I wanted to buffer all my points so I made sure the *Use only selected* was unchecked. I had to decide on a *buffer distance*. I browsed to save and named my new shapefile. There were buffers around the points, but I wasn't sure if I liked the buffers created, so I right clicked on it in the *Layers Panel* and clicked *Remove*. I started again, adjusted the buffer distance and overwrote my old file by saving it in the same place with the same name (Figure 5.7, on the next page).

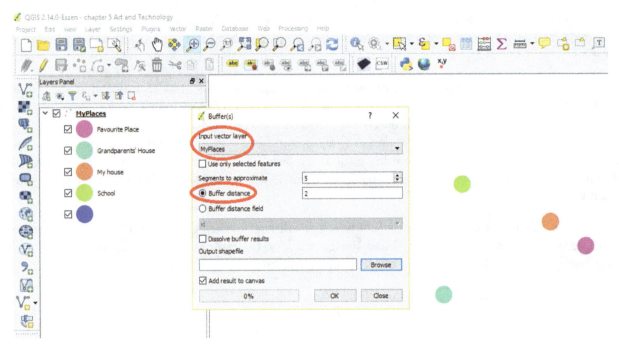

Figure 5.7:

I dragged the BufferPlaces under the MyPlaces layer so the points would draw over the buffers (Figure 5.8).

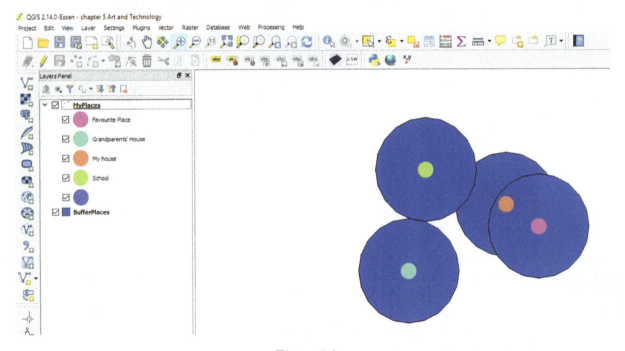

Figure 5.8:

I saw there were lots of things that could be done with buffers and colours and with markers and colours.

Just give it a try, I encouraged myself. I read more about how to work with symbology in the *QGIS User Guide: Vector Layers: The Symbol Library* and then I just started clicking and experimenting (Figure 5.9).

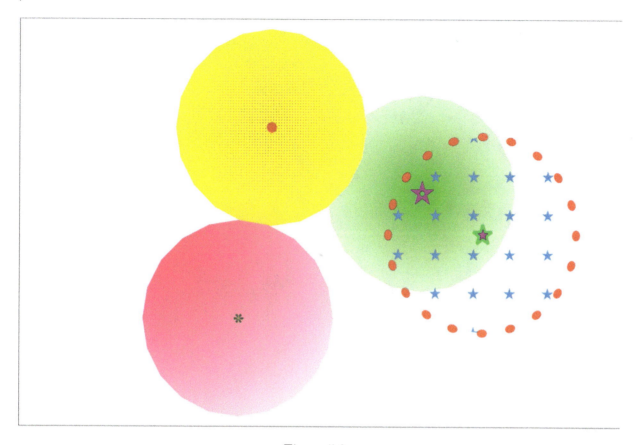

Figure 5.9:

I looked at my map. I liked it. Would anyone know it was even a map if I didn't tell them? All I needed was a title. Mapping my places. Feelings and places. Thoughts about space and time. What do you think? What would you call your map?

> Don't forget to record what you use in your Concept Map. By now your Concept Map should be looking pretty good!

6. Flight Path

"There's trouble, captain."

I looked over at my sergeant, so tired I was having trouble seeing him next to me in the dusk. I stretched out one side of my body after the other and waited for the muscles to snap back into place. "What kind of trouble?" I asked, hoping that he was over exaggerating the situation as he so often did. He was always too excited by his job and always too willing to put in the extra hours that would turn an ordinary day's journey into a carefully orchestrated performance of perfection.

"I've done the calculations several times and each time I come up with the same results," he said. "We have to change our route for more than one leg of the journey over the next few days. It won't be easy to avoid all of the regular barriers to the flight path as well as to find food and comfortable accommodations for the group."

Oh, for the days when we just flew south for the winter, I thought. The days when there was room for everyone to land for the night, food to be had, open skies, starry nights. Yes, there were head winds and rain, sometimes even snow to contend with, but there weren't the pressures that we faced now. Lack of starlight from light pollution, lack of sunlight from smog, hunters everywhere, poised to shoot as we took off or landed in the far too few fields that were left for us from the spread of cities everywhere. Quite frankly, the thought was so depressing I often would rather not know what we faced. I shook my head, saddened that being a leader had become such a burden. Yes, having this new Sergeant was a wonderful thing, what with all his technical skills and abilities and that wonderful new idea he had brought back from a meeting with another group, enabling him to use the keyboard much more effectively than before. Whoever would have thought something as simple as a stick held in the beak would make data input and query so much easier? As a leader, I was ashamed I had not thought of it, but my thoughts were in the clouds it seemed, pinned to the past and my memories of happier times. Really, I berated myself, I must catch up to this new way of doing things.

"Okay, Sergeant," I said, "Tell me what the trouble is. Better yet, show me on the map."

"Right, Ma'am," he settled the mobile device in front of me. "Let me show you what I've got. I call it NOIR."

"Noir?" I asked, puzzled.

"Acronym, Ma'am," he explained. "It stands for Nominal, Ordinal, Interval, and Ratio. It means "black" in French. I thought it was a good way to remember it, seeing as how we are Black Brant Geese."

Ever since he met that group of French geese last year on the coast, he hadn't stopped thinking about France, talking about France, using French technology. Always something new, I sighed. Then I became impatient with myself again. What was wrong with me, why was I always thinking about the past and not willing to embrace the future and the most modern ways. The sergeant was not at fault, I was. Not to mention that the French geese had a leader who made me feel totally inadequate, a leader with all of the latest mobile technology.

"Good acronym," I agreed, as much to convince myself as to be agreeable with him. "Now show me what it means on the map. Let's get this flight path sorted and get our group to a nice spot for the winter."

"First I put the names of all of the cities and towns on the map," he said. "That is Nominal data. To do that, you label the map with the names. In French, name is nom." He pointed at the paper between us with his beak. "I got this data from the French geese. I copied down the pieces I thought we would need from their maps. These names are really old. Look at this one", he said, tapping it with his beak, "called Turn. In the old days we used to turn when we passed it so we could get to the next safe place." He shook his head. "It isn't that way anymore. The area around there is just scary with hunters and all pavement now." We both closed our eyes, partly to block it out and partly to remember what the old geese had told us of the wonderful days, long gone. "Still, the names help us so that we can talk about areas and be sure we know we are talking about the same place."

"Next," he said, "I ordered the cities by size and made the dots that represent them larger or smaller based on the number of people. Look," he pointed, "this is easily the biggest city, based on population, but it doesn't tell us exactly how large the city is in terms of city boundaries. Still, it helps a bit. The bigger the city, the more likely we won't find food."

I looked at the size of the dots. He was right, it helped, but it wasn't perfect.

"It also doesn't tell us how much bigger one city is than another. The cities are ordered, that is the Ordinal part of NOIR."

I puzzled a bit over that, wanting some time to think, but he went on.

"Next I mapped the Interval data. For this I used population again. I grouped the cities using a method called Natural Breaks. There are five groups. Now, instead of 20 cities, we can look at five colours and judge what areas are likely to be a problem. Captain," he shrugged, "my reasoning was this, with more people there would be more danger."

"A guess, but that seems as if it might be a useful way to look at the numbers," I agreed. He looked relieved, happy to accept the praise.

"I was thinking that, the darker the colour, the more people living there. So, on my map, darker means that area should be avoided. What do you think?" He pointed at the map. "These are the places we likely need to avoid at all costs."

Lack of good places to land and lack of food were one thing, I thought, but a day without them was not the same as a day with hunters. We could go on, tired and hungry. But there was no going on after... I shuddered thinking about what might be if we were not very careful in our planning.

"And finally, Ratio data," he said. "With this colour," he pointed, "you can see how many hunters there are relative to the number of people. I found out from one of the geese we met last year..." he paused. I knew what was coming. "In France, there is a database of hunters. I copied down the numbers to add to our table. Sometimes there are lots of people and lots of hunters, but sometimes there are not that many people but lots of hunters. It's a good thing to know."

"Okay," I agreed. "Now what do we do with all this information?"

"Captain," he said with conviction, "we map our route."

"Do we need help?" I asked.

"As much as we can get," he answered. "I'll send everyone the data table they need to do the work. Data driven mapping," he said, his eyes snapping with excitement, "is what it's all about. The French geese said. . ."

I didn't give him the time to finish. I turned to the flock. "Now, Mapping Recruits, here is your job. Use the table the Sergeant will send you to add the information he has already put on his map. Use. . ." I hesitated.

"The NOIR method," he whispered.

"NOIR," I repeated, "then, find the best route for us to negotiate the hazards and find the best wintering spot ever. We need ideas. We need your input. Let's get to work!", I cheered them on.

"Best place ever!" they responded.

_____

You might not be an expert, but do your best to help. The geese are counting on you. Where should the geese go? What path should they follow? After you map everything, evaluate the areas for hunters and size of city. Where do you think they should stay for the winter?

Note: A special message from the Sergeant: DO NOT follow the placement of the points on the example map. Why not? I'll tell you. The Sergeant mentioned that he was given a photo by a goose who was reporting a problem. The photo was of the example map and a goose, Honkers. The Sergeant was not surprised by the photo, showing Honkers asleep beside his mobile device when he was supposed to be working on his map. Pragmatically, the sergeant cut the sleeping Honkers out so that he could use the map for illustrating the process, below, but you will not want to copy the work.

"That Honkers," said the Sergeant, "probably just sprayed the dots on the map and then went to sleep. Thanks for taking the photo," he said to the reporting goose. "Honkers is never going to move up in the flight line ranks at this rate but at least the photo is useful for showing the others what could be done, and what NOT to do!."

Create a new shapefile layer. *Layer: Create Layer: New Shapefile Layer*. *Save* it and give it a name.

Click on the *Pencil tool* to go into edit mode.

Put 20 dots in the map panel (you will decide where they should be) and give them the number 1-20 for ID as you create them. Your location choice is your own. Remember, don't follow Honkers' map, Figure 6.1, on the following page!

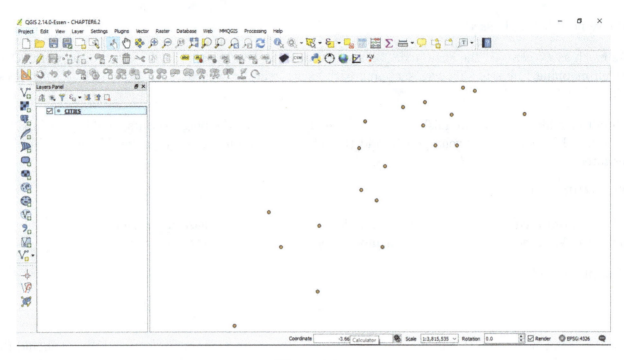

Figure 6.1:

Now, using the table in Figure 6.2, right click on the layer and *Open Attribute Table*. Find the *New Field tool* and add a new field: `Cityname`, Type: `Text data`, Length: `80`. Populate it using the data table.

Add another New field: Name: `Population`, Type: `Whole number`, Length: `10` and type in the numbers from the table.

Add another New field, Name: `Hunters`, Type: `Whole number`, Length: `10`. Populate it using the table. See Figure 6.3.

Save your edits. *Close* the *Attribute Table*.

ID	CITYNAME	POPULATION	HUNTERS
1	SWEETWATER	90000	185
2	CROWDED	500000	8000
3	AVOID	1000450	65000
4	NECESSARY	350000	2000
5	TURN	75000	60
6	SMALLFIELD	6000	70
7	FOXES	3500	320
8	CRESCENTMOON	100000	2000
9	MUDFIELD	5000	1000
10	HEADWIND	20000	88
11	GREATGRASS	5500	300
12	COWRESIDUE	200	10
13	PINKSKY	450	12
14	SEEDSGALORE	35000	1500
15	SALTYWATER	680	22
16	SADLOSS	880	60
17	ALMOSTTHERE	1000	69
18	DONTSTOPNOW	3000	190
19	TAILWIND	100	35
20	WINTERHOME	10800	5

Figure 6.2:

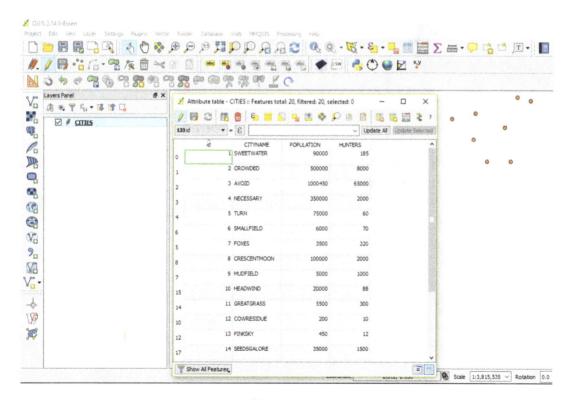

Figure 6.3:

Right click on the layer and click on *Duplicate* twice to create two additional layers so you can represent the data in different ways—that is, you will follow the NOIR method the Sergeant detailed.

In the original layer, right click, click on *Properties: Labels*. Choose *Show all labels for this layer*, *Label with* CityName, in *Rendering* check the box to *Show Labels for All* in case some are left out because they overlap each other. This is the "N" part of NOIR, the nominal (Figure 6.4).

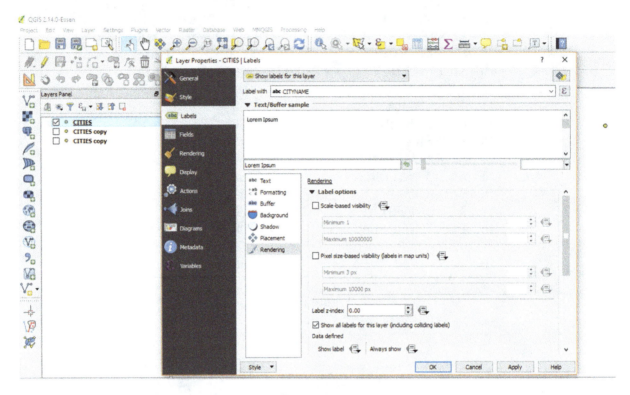

Figure 6.4:

In the first copy of the layer, right click on it and select *Properties: Style*, use *Graduated*, *Column* is Population, *Method* is *Size*. *Size from* is 0.05 to 8.0, *Mode* is *Quantile (Equal Count)*, *Classes* is 20. Click *Classify*. This will give you a different size dot for each city's population. This is the "O" part of NOIR, the ordinal (Figure 6.5, on the facing page).

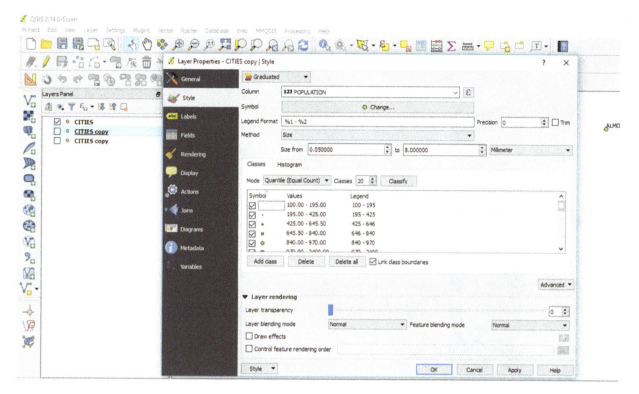

Figure 6.5:

In the second copy of the first layer, right click on the layer and select *Properties: Style*, use *Graduated*, *Column* is Population, *Method* is *Colour*, *Mode* is *Natural Breaks (Jenks)*, *Classes 5* and click *Classify*. Experiment with other Modes and numbers of classes, if you like. See what happens, see if you can understand the data better with other modes and with other numbers of classes. This is the "I" part of NOIR, the interval (Figure 6.6, on the next page).

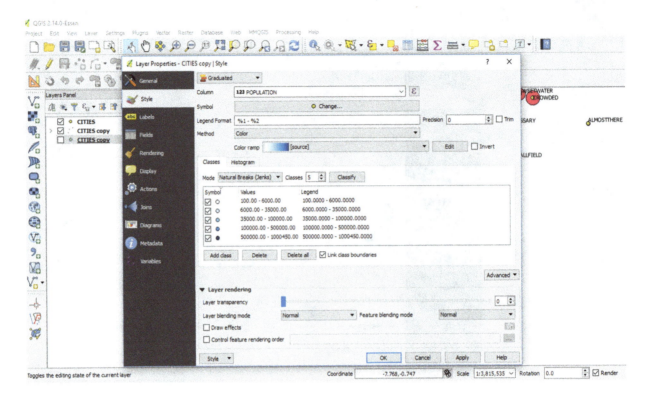

Figure 6.6:

You will need to reorder the layers by dragging them up and down in the layer list and/or making them visible and not, to see the different ways to look.

In one layer, it doesn't matter which, right click and select *Properties: Diagrams*, check the box for *Show diagrams for this layer*. Select *Diagram Type Pie chart*. Click on Population, click on the "*+*" sign to add it to the *Assigned attributes*. Click on Hunters, click on the "*+*" sign to add it to the *Assigned attributes*. Click *Apply*. Now you have the "R" part of NOIR, the ratio. See Figure 6.7, on the facing page and Figure 6.8, on the next page.

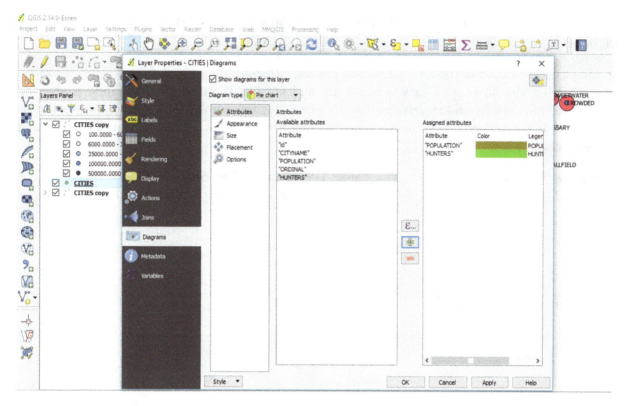

Figure 6.7:

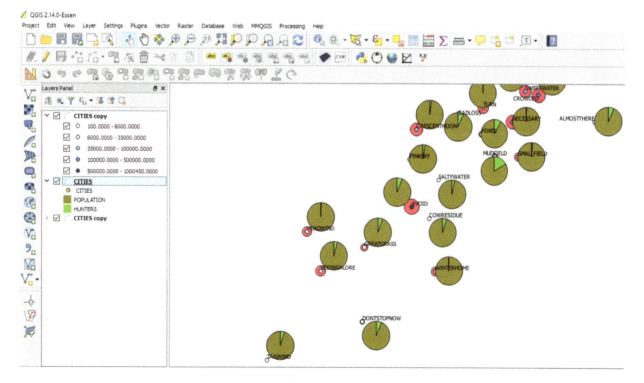

Figure 6.8:

Arrange the layers so that they show the data in the best way, or turn the layers on and off using the check boxes. You decide how you can work best with the data.

Read about Classification in the *QGIS Training Manual: Module: Classifying Vector Data/Lesson: Classification*. Being able to analyse data is important and not just to geese. Being a good analyst means being able to think clearly and creatively. It isn't easy and it takes practice, but you have to start somewhere! Check it out online (search for Nominal, Ordinal, Interval, Ratio—maybe watch a video) and see what else you can learn.

Examine the flight path possibilities. Use *Layer: Create Layer: New Shapefile Layer*. Create a new line shapefile and digitize the route you think the geese should take. They will be thankful for your help!

7. Group Work Groan

"I already know what is going to happen when I say this," said our teacher, "but I'm going to say it anyway. Today we start a new unit and we are going to work through it in groups."

We groaned, collectively.

"See," she said, "I knew it. Groaning about group work. Exactly what I thought you would do. Well," she went on, "why not go for the full deal and get a really loud groan from all of you?" she looked at us, almost laughing at what she knew would happen after her next announcement. "This will be group work where I assign you to groups and, as you will see, I have carefully selected groups so none of you will be working with the people you usually work with." She looked around, smiling, waiting—the groans had stopped and the low noise was replaced with pointed looks of terror as we flashed our eyes at each other, wondering what this was all about. How cruel could she be?

Now, I for one, did not mind our teacher. I did think that her heart was in the right place. She wanted us to learn and she sometimes looked as if she was in pain, or even sad, when we failed to live up to expectations or couldn't answer questions on tests. She did try hard to get our interest and to help us whenever she could. Sometimes though, for some of us, myself included, her efforts just weren't enough to make the grade, so to speak. I just couldn't muster interest in some of the things we needed to study. I wondered what she was letting us in for this time. Did she really think mixing us up into groups where we didn't feel we belonged would help us with our learning? I listened with some interest, in spite of myself. What did she have planned? More to the point, why?

"Please look at the list I am handing out and move yourself to a table with the rest of your group. On the papers, next to the list of group members, I have written a challenge for your group. You have one week to complete the challenge." She passed out papers and sat down at her desk. The room was quiet. "Well," she said, "what are you waiting for? GO! Get started."

I waited until a paper was passed to me, scanned down the list to find my name and read the names of the others in my group. Oh, my goodness! I gulped. I was really mixed in. I had barely ever spoken to one of the girls with whom I would need to work. She was in the "super cool" group in the class—the ones who had the best of everything. I had never spoken to one of the boys, who, to my knowledge, had never even spoken to anyone in the class. Not ever. The other two I had known since I was in my first year of school. I had never been friendly with them though. Yes, indeed, the teacher had done a fine job, at least for my group, of making sure I would be working with virtual strangers. And what was the challenge she assigned? Under the list of our names, I read, "Make a map of an area you know nothing about. Make the map look different from any we have worked on so far. Write the instructions so anyone looking at your map can make the same one."

I exhaled slowly. A few people in the class were moving already. I grabbed my things and moved to the corner of the room to watch what the others would do. After a few minutes, noting that my group was not organising, I went to a table that was nearly empty and called, "Emily! Mac! Over here." That got their attention and they stood up and started to move. "Jonathan! Bobbi!", I said loudly enough for them to hear over the noise of chairs scraping and chattering, "Come and sit over here." I wondered what I was doing being the organiser. It was not really my strength, but I thought we might as well get started and get it over with.

Everyone sat. Plunked in their seats, they slouched and waited. All except for Bobbi who whipped out her mobile and searched the Internet. "Just a second," she said, and walked quickly to the teacher's desk. "Is it okay if we use our devices in class?" she asked.

The teacher nodded, "Good idea," she answered. "You might need to do some quick searches initially before you get onto the PCs."

Bobbi came back and showed us her search string: "Group work, how to succeed." Not a bad idea, I thought. She read a bit and then put it on the table, turned it so we could see the title. "Forming, Storming, Norming, Performing", I read.

"My parents have talked about this before, at home," she admitted. "They talk about having to work in teams in their offices. They say everyone has trouble with team work but you can get better at it if you try." She raised her eyebrows at us and tilted her head to one side.

"I'm willing to give it a go", I said.

Emily and Mac nodded. Jonathan looked at the floor. We left him alone. He didn't disagree so that was good enough for now. I said, hopefully, "Maybe we can get past the Storming part and get right to the Performing. After all, a week isn't a long time to get something done that is new to all of us." Nods all around the table made me feel more cheerful about our prospects.

"Okay," said Mac. "Let's start by picking an area we know nothing about. Ummm. . .", he drummed his fingers on the table. "Some place in China," he suggested. "Nobody has been there, right?"

"None of us," said Emily, "but there are people in the class who are from China, I think."

"True," said Bobbi. "How about. . ."

"How about Tajikistan?" Jonathan surprised us all by looking up from his hands, knotted on the table in front of him. His voice was high and squeaky. He looked and sounded like a frightened mouse.

"Sounds great," I enthused, partly because I was so glad he had joined in and partly because I thought it was a good suggestion. I had never even heard of that place, let alone knew where it was.

"It was part of the former Soviet Union," he said, very quietly now. I could tell he was nervous about talking to the group. "There are a lot of mountains. It could make a really interesting map."

"Why would it be interesting?" I asked at the same time Mac stated, "I think we should stick to something we know a bit better, something we at least have an idea about. New, but not entirely unknown," he expanded, "Something where we don't have to spend all of our time researching before we get to work."

Bobbi thought about what we both said, and asked, "Yeah, why would it be interesting to map mountains?"

"Because," Jonathan said, "we could use rasters."

"What?" all four asked, practically in unison.

"It's a different kind of map," he explained. "Here," he put his hand carefully towards Bobbi's mobile. "Can I?" he asked. She pushed it at him.

He searched for a minute and then showed us the results, images from his search. The images looked great. They looked like works of art, not like maps. I was sold. Bobbi and Emily looked impressed. Only Mac scowled a bit, still not convinced that it would just be too difficult to do but, "Okay," he said, "if you know how and if you can show us, I'm in."

Was that our only "Storming", I thought? Could we really get away with that little fighting in our group? Best not to get too excited too soon, I thought. A week was a long time.

"So," I said to Jonathan, "tell us what you think we need to do."

Jonathan, far from being the retiring, quiet, shy person I expected him to be, took charge and began ordering us around. He ordered quietly, but there was no mistaking that his statements were orders. He was so sure of himself now that he knew what he was doing and the rest of us needed to follow. I wondered how long it would take until someone got annoyed. I hoped he knew how to lead as well as knowing about mapping mountains.

"I already know how to do this," he stated, "so I will look in the manuals for pages that help. Bobbi, you could use the camera on your phone to take photos of the screens that come up while the map is being created. We can put the images into the document that tells people how to create the map. Mac, you and Emily can write the instructions down, as I tell you how to make the map." He looked at me. "You can make the map," he said.

"Hold on," said Mac. "It might be your idea, but that doesn't make you the leader of the group. I say we have a vote for leader."

"I think," I said, "we should look for volunteers for the different jobs. Let people decide what they would like to do. Maybe we should list the jobs first."

Emily said, "I like writing. I would be good at putting the instructions together. But it would be good to have someone working with me so I don't miss anything."

"I take pictures with my phone all the time," said Bobbi. "Photographer, that's me."

So far Jonathan's plan was being accepted. I sighed. Working with software was not my forte. I was much better at reading about theory than doing the technical work. Still, Jonathan was right. He did know how to do it, so having him looking at the manual for extra ideas might be good. "Okay," I agreed, "I'll work with the software." It's always good to stretch yourself, I said to allay my fears that were hovering like irritating flies around my thoughts. Give it a try. You can do it, I cheered silently to myself.

We all looked at Mac. He snorted a bit. Actually, it sounded more like a growl, but he nodded, rolling his eyes. "Okay. I'll work on instructions with Emily."

Jonathan pulled up the manuals online and searched for the right chapter. I opened up the mapping program, waiting for instructions. Emily and Mac sat at their laptops with blank documents, ready to start typing. Bobbi fiddled with her camera settings.

> Follow along with the team to create a raster map, but deviate from their ideas as soon as you like. Maybe your data would be better presented in a different way. Maybe you just prefer other methods. Don't forget to add to your Concept Map as you work through the menus and icons.

"Okay. First we need a raster. We need to find and download one from the Internet. There is lots of free data. Go to the Internet browser and search for data with the right format," said Jonathan.

"What is the right format?" I asked.

"Good question," he said. Click on *Layers: Add Layer: Add Raster Layer*. Click where it says, *Add files (*)*. See the list. Those are the kinds of formats we can use. Lots of them. Do a search and download one that has a file extension like the list. For example, we can use a Digital Elevation Model (DEM). In the QGIS User Guide, there is a chapter on *Working with Raster Data*. In the Training Manual, there is *Module: Rasters, Lesson: Working with Raster Data*. We should read about those first. The second thing to do is to find a raster and the second is to click on *Layers: Add Layer: Add Raster Layer*."

> Note: You can find rasters on the Internet that are available for free if you have permissions to download data. If you do not, ask your teacher to provide one. A good site to look at is Web GIS, http://www.webgis.com/, Digital Terrain.

"Go slower," said Mac. "I can't type that fast."

"I'll type," said Emily. "You watch what she does on the laptop and what he reads from the manual and then you check what I've written." It sounded a bit like an order and I could see Mac struggling with it, but he nodded again, seeing the sense in it.

Emily typed. I followed the instructions and the raster showed up. Bobbi took a photo (Figure 7.1, on the facing page).

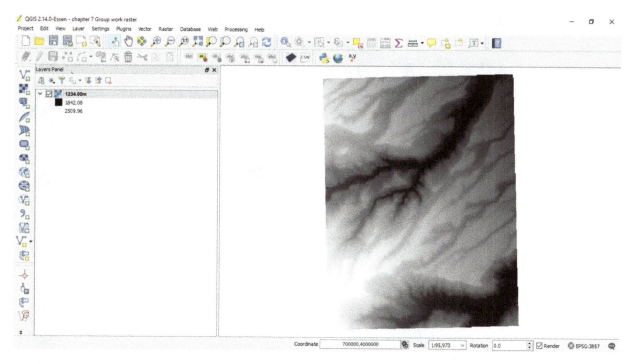

Figure 7.1:

"Okay, what we have here is a singleband grey."

"How do you know?"

"Because the User Guide says that QGIS will use that method to render if it is not multiband. Render means draw. But we will want to change that. We can make it singleband, pseudocolour."

"Why do we want to do that?"

"Because it is more interesting than grey and we want to explore what we can do, not just take the default," Jonathan explained. "We need to look at the Properties. Right click on the *Layer* and select *Properties*."

"Now, note down the min and max numbers. We may want them if we decide to change things later. Take a screenshot, Bobbi" (Figure 7.2, on the next page).

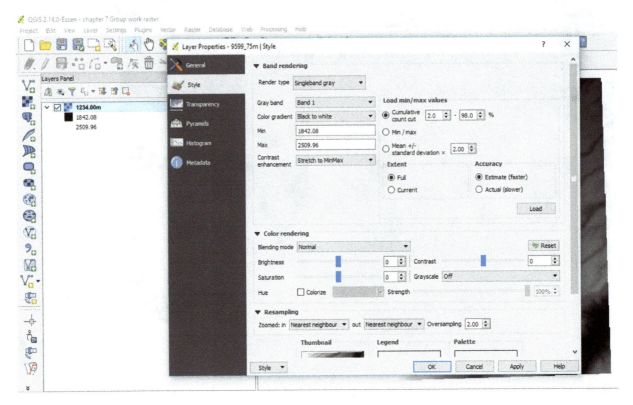

Figure 7.2:

"Select *Singleband pseudocolour*, *Mode: Equal Interval*, *Classes* 5 and *Classify*." I clicked as fast as I could. "Screenshot," he ordered (Figure 7.3, on the facing page).

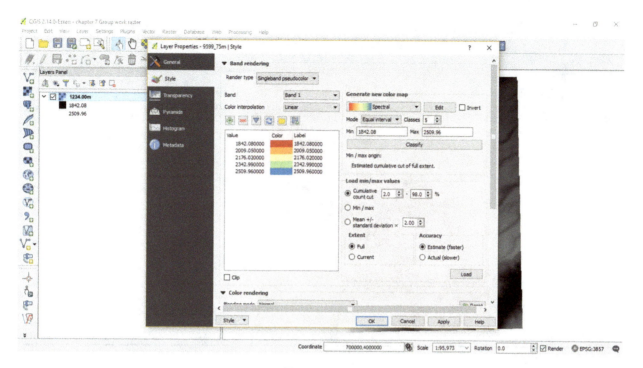

Figure 7.3:

"Neat," said Mac. "But the rivers are red."

"We can make them blue. Go back to *Properties* and check *Invert*. Now *Classify* again."

I like it," said Mac.

I don't," said Bobbi. "I liked the other colours better. What if we had more colours? Twelve classes instead of 5?" I made it be 12.

"No", said Mac. "How about 12 and use grey again?" I made the changes.

"No, said Bobbi. "It was better with the colours, I agree."

I made it be 5 classes and *Spectral* again for the colour map. Then, while there was a lull in the orders and opinions, I used the *Zoom in* Tool, zoomed into the raster, and saw all of the little square pixels.

"Use the *Identify* tool", instructed Jonathan. I found the tool and clicked on a square.

"Catch that Bobbi," he said. "See the number. That is the value for that pixel. The elevation at that location" (Figure 7.4, on the next page).

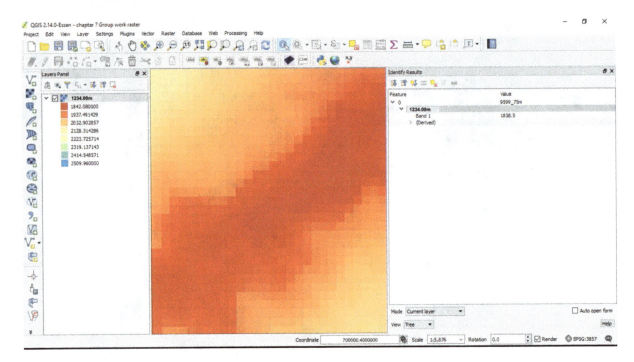

Figure 7.4:

I clicked around on a few more pixels and then saw at the bottom of the screen that there was a dropdown menu that said *View*. The choices were *Tree*, *Table* and *Graph*. Each time I clicked I was rewarded with a different view of what the pixel looked like from the data point of view. Everyone looked on, eager to see what would happen after each click.

I closed down the window, right clicked on the *Layer* and selected *Zoom to Layer* so that the raster was the same as before.

"Okay, let's do one more thing," said Jonathan. "We'll use the QGIS Training Manual this time. We're going to create a hillshade." Bobbi got ready to snap a shot. I got ready to click the buttons, Emily was still busy typing and correcting. Mac was enjoying shifting between all of our stations and looking over our shoulders.

"Just a minute," he said, reading the instructions Emily had typed. "Okay, all good." He gave the thumbs up and Jonathan started reading again.

"Go to the *Raster Menu Item: Analysis: DEM (Terrain Models)*. Bobbi, shoot," he instructed. (Figure 7.5, on the facing page).

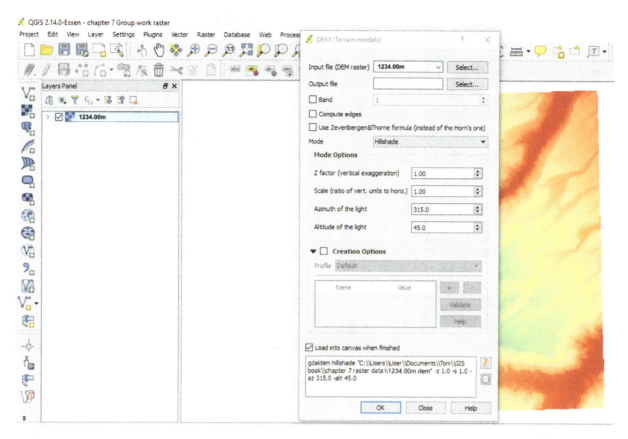

Figure 7.5:

"Have a look at the dialogue box. See the part for *Vertical Exaggeration*. Make it be 10. We can make these mountains look even higher than they are," Jonathan smiled to himself. "Let's make them better than the Himalayas."

I laughed and changed the number. Then I clicked on *Select* beside the *Output File*, browsed to a good location and named my file. I clicked on *Save* and then I clicked okay.

"Did you get that Emily?" asked Mac.

"Just a minute," she said. "Was it name the file and then change to 10?"

"Other way around," said Jonathan, "but we can test it later."

"Good idea," said Mac. "If someone else tests the instructions we can be sure we got it right. I can do that," he offered.

"Okay we need to make sure the hillshade is on top of the raster in the Layers Panel. Click on it and drag it to the top. Draw order is important," he said. "Then we need to set the transparency of the hillshade."

I right clicked on the hillshade layer and chose *Properties* and then clicked on *Transparency*. I changed it to 25 and we looked. Bobbi said, "Make it 75 transparent." I did. She took a shot (Figure 7.6, on the next page).

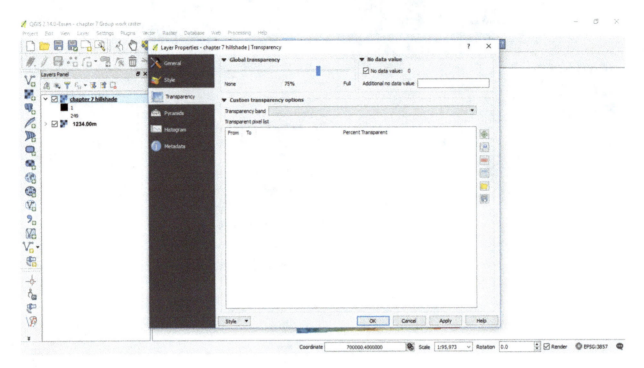

Figure 7.6:

"Now that looks interesting," I said. I clicked off the check box of the hillshade so that we could see the raster with and without. Definitely more interesting with. Bobbi took a photo (Figure 7.7).

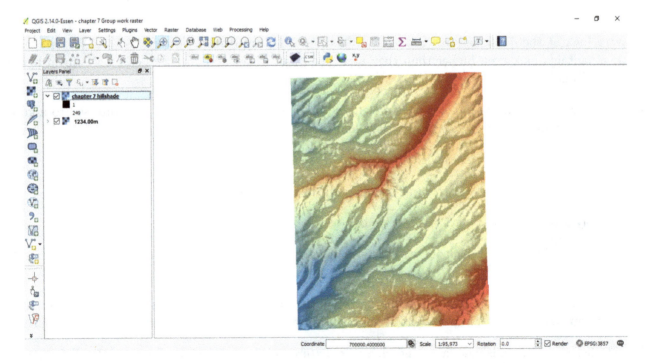

Figure 7.7:

"I still think we could do more with the colours," said Bobbi.

"I agree," said Mac. "Want to play around with them for a while?" he asked her.

"I'm going to do some more reading to see what else we can do," said Jonathan.

"I'll investigate too," I said, happy to relinquish the controls.

"I'll keep on taking notes," said Emily.

We all smiled at each other. Forming, storming, norming, performing. Yes, I thought, we had reached the performing stage. Best group ever!

8. The Magic of Mapping

Do you believe in magic? I know what you are thinking about me when I ask that. She's nuts, you're thinking. Who believes in magic? What is she thinking about when she says 'magic'? Fairies, witches, charms, spells, elves?

Sure it sounds a bit crazy, even to me, but still I wonder. I wonder about all the books people write about magic, not just for little kids, but for adults too. Books about fantasy times and fantasy places. Not just science fiction about what the world might be like in the future when we use science to invent strange, new things, but about things that are here, right now, in our world. Things we don't pay attention to. Things we don't even see anymore. Things we don't believe in because we only believe in the explanations for things science gives us. But what if science is just a way of explaining things that isn't so different from the way people used to explain things with magic. After all, when it comes right down to it, we can't explain science.

Scientists explain the world by saying it is made up of things we can't see, powered by things we can't see, and, in the end, even the scientists have to say they suspect some things happen or some things exist because otherwise their theories don't make sense. They still can't answer things like: why does gravity work or whether light is a wave or a particle? Or give answers to things that maybe aren't so important, like: why do we yawn or why do cats purr? The atomic theory has been accepted for so long that we see it as truth rather than a theory, but there are parts of it that are surely strange. Atoms are the smallest things scientists said. Then, no, scientists announced they had discovered quarks which are smaller still. But what are quarks—has anyone one seen one?

Science is okay to talk about and to teach in schools—everyone seems to agree with each other on that. But magic is not okay, it is crazy and not many want to talk about it, let alone discuss it, especially not in school. I'm not so sure though. At least with magic you don't pretend to know everything. Magic leaves doors open.

I know I don't know everything. And, truth be told, I'm okay with that. I like a little surprise in my life. I like to think that magical things are awaiting me if I have the eyes to see them. And I look—look every day for magic to peek out at me and for me to escape from the bland kind of life where for every question there is a 'factual' answer—answers that have had most of the fun stripped right out of them.

At least with magic there is wonder. Sure, scientists wonder about things. They wonder and then they get out their graduated cylinders, and their calculators, and their rulers. If they wonder about something, they want to find a way to measure it and figure it out so they can stop wondering. They don't want to wonder and feel the wonder and experience something as being wonderful. They want wonder to be explained. Me, I just want to be able to feel it.

So how did I feel when I went into class and was told that I was going to make a map of my favourite place in the world. Discouraged at first. I would have to take a place that I thought was full of wonder and stuff it into a computer program. There would be nothing left of the wonder after it was mangled by software and depicted with a digital image. Taking the easy way out was always an option. I could map my street and write something about my home being the best place in the world. Who could argue? And I already knew that making a street map would be easy. A few labels, a photo, and some nice flourishes of colour would complete the work. I could just imagine handing in the work and getting back a grade, being done with it. Easy—too easy. Maybe I was getting a bit tired of easy. Maybe I wanted to do something different, to show I was different. Maybe I should put a bit of magic into my work. . .

Now, you are thinking: she is REALLY crazy. How is she going to put magic into a map? True, I stopped talking to myself for a minute—I would have to give that some thought.

On my way home, as I looked out beyond the edge of my neighbourhood to the mountains, looking at the trees, the purple of the heather and the darker rock above, where nothing grew, I thought about the mountains and how they really were my favourite place. The mountains were where I really felt at home.

I was never frightened there, when I walked by myself, not like I was when I walked home at night from my friends' houses, along the streets, wondering if there were any nasty people around. I knew being in the mountains could be dangerous, but at least it was a danger I felt I had control of. If I was careful, I knew I would be okay. On the streets, bad things could happen. The noise of the cars was unpleasant. The feel of the pavement under my feet was hard and unyielding. The air smelled.

In the mountains, the air was sweet, there was no sound and then suddenly the sound of the wind in the plants, or the sound of insects keeping time with each other, or the sound of birds. The paths were softer, fainter, beckoning.

I could make a map of the mountains, I thought, that would be more of the truth about me and what I really loved. But how? How could I show them in a way that wasn't just about facts: a name, a measurement of height, a precise location. That was something I would need to investigate. How could a map show the magic of the mountains?

I knew maps could be pretty, beautiful even. That was the job of the cartographer. The cartographer represented the content that the map was trying to communicate, using the best layout, colours and classifications, for example. I looked at some websites on cartography and cartographic conventions to see what others had done. Then I read something interesting on one of the pages.

There was a distinction between qualitative and quantitative research. The website said that quantitative research was about the numbers and about measurement. Qualitative research was about how people felt, but it was descriptive, not about statistics.

Now I thought I was onto something. I wanted a qualitative map, not just cartographically qualitative, like a thematic map, but qualitative content that was about feelings. I wondered how I could do that. I wondered if anyone else had ever tried. A quick search showed that others had interest in Qualitative GIS. I found a book about it. That was inspiration enough for me. I was going to see what I could come up with.

I thought about what I wanted to communicate with my map. I wanted to tell others that the mountains were a place of great importance to me. To show that, I thought of using contrast, contrasting what was important with what was less important. Right now, the only two other places that really had importance to me, constantly, were school and home. How did I feel about them? Sometimes I liked school, sometimes I didn't. Home was my safe place, but not always exciting, not always perfect either.

I could show how I felt about the places in my life with points on the map. I had read about the two different ways to think about mapping. One way was with vectors—that was discrete data. It showed a point, for example, and the area that was not points or lines or polygons, wasn't really anything (Figure 8.1).

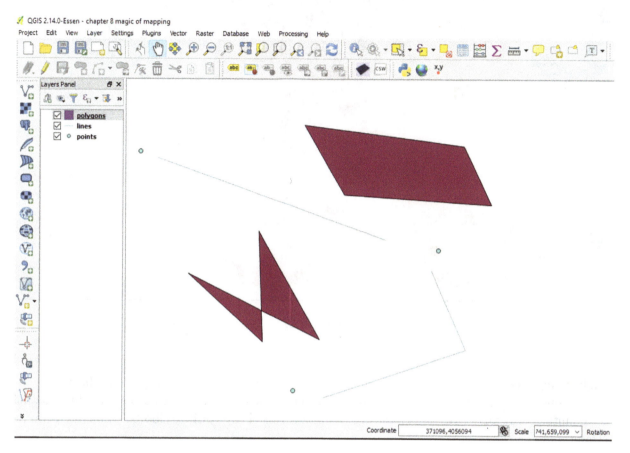

Figure 8.1:

The other way to represent maps was as a continuous surface, as a raster. With a raster, the world was covered with data, data that was in a grid. Each pixel of the grid had a value associated with it (Figure 8.2, on the following page).

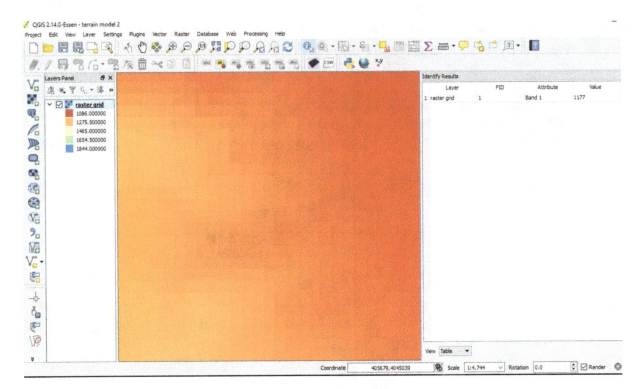

Figure 8.2:

I thought using the raster might give me more scope for how I wanted to represent the places in my world. Not one point for the school, but raster cells that showed the ups and downs. Not just the height of the mountain, but where the places on the mountain raised my spirits. Good, I thought, I am on to something.

First thing I needed was to create a new point shapefile of my house, the mountains and my school, *Layer: Create Layer: New Shapefile Layer*. Select *Point* as the type. *Save* the file and give it a name. Select the *Pencil* tool to toggle editing and *Add Feature*. I gave each feature an ID. I toggled editing off by clicking on the *Pencil* again and *Saved*.

Now I needed to make an empty grid. Then I would add a point to each square of the grid. The point would already have an X, Y coordinate because all mapping does. X gives a measure of the location in the horizontal (East and West) and Y gives a location in the vertical (North and South). But there is another dimension, and that is elevation. To work with 3D (E/W, N/S and height) I needed Z as well. I would add a Z value to the point which would give height. Then I would make the grid points into a Digital Elevation Model which would draw as a raster. I could use a QGIS plugin to give the raster 3D.

To make the grid: *Vector: Research Tools: Vector Grid*. The *Grid Extent* was my points shapefile. I chose *Update Extents from Layer*. That would make my grid cover the area described by Points.shp.

The X Min and X Max described the coordinates of the lower left and lower right corners of the grid. If I subtracted the min from the max, I would get the number of squares along the bottom of the grid. I did not want to deal with thousands and thousands. I decided to change the Parameters for X, Y so I would get a reasonable number of grid cells to work with.

So, I changed the default *Parameters* from .0001 to 500. I didn't want the grid to have really, tiny squares as it would take a long time to draw. If the area I was working with was very large and the grid more than 40 squares, it would be too big to work with. A grid of more than 40 might need the number 500 to be adjusted until it was right.

I clicked *Browse* in *Output Shapefile* to find a place to save my file. I named the file and then I clicked okay (Figure 8.3).

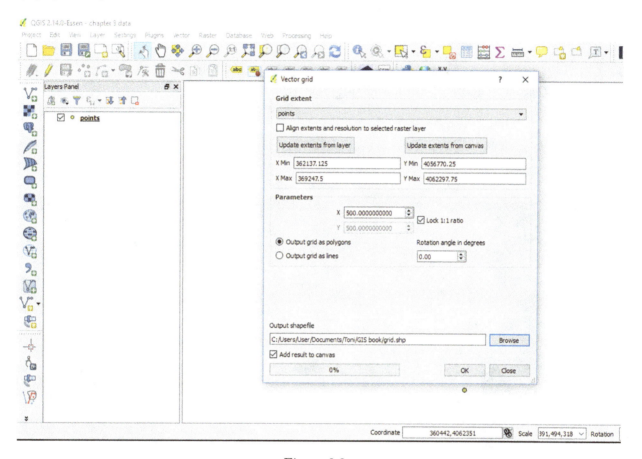

Figure 8.3:

Now for a point in the middle of each polygon. I didn't want to have to put a point in each manually, so I searched and found there was a tool to do it for me. I used *Vector: Geometry Tools: Polygon Centroids*.

Now I had to add a field to the table for elevation, the Z value. I right clicked on the layer and chose *Open Attribute Table*. I toggled on the editing for that layer with the *Pencil Tool*. I clicked on the icon for *Add a Field*. I named it Z.

Using the dropdown menu for the tool *Select Features*, I changed it to *Select Features by Polygon*. I drew a polygon around the points that represent the mountain area. The polygon was a strange shape! In the *Attribute Table*, I clicked on the tool that allows you to *Move selection to top*. I clicked in the Z field and added the values that represented the areas on the map. I did the same for home and school. I chose to use numbers that ranged from 20 to 10,000. Not the height of the land or the building, but a number that represented some of the dots in the grids. A few low points and some midrange for school. A few higher numbers for home and some really large numbers for areas in the mountains. I experimented with values until I thought they represented how I felt.

I used the *Deselect Features Tool*. Now I selected the rows that had no values and put 0 in them all. Stop editing by toggling the *Pencil* tool. I *Saved*. I closed the *Attribute Table*.

Next on the list was creating a TIN, a triangulated irregular network. I used *Raster: Interpolation*. I used the *Input* Centroid Layer, *Interpolation Attribute* Z and clicked on *OK*. I saved it to a file with the name TIN.

I decided to experiment with colour, using *Properties: Style*. I filled in the parameters: *Singleband Pseudocolour, Linear, Spectral*. I changed the *Max* to be the number of the highest value used. I selected *Equal Interval*, *Classes 20* and clicked *Classify* (Figure 8.4).

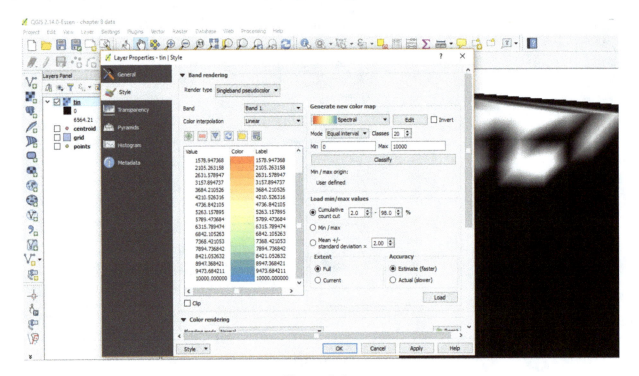

Figure 8.4:

My map was interesting. I could see the mountain was more prominent, but the locations of my house and school didn't reveal much (Figure 8.5, on the next page).

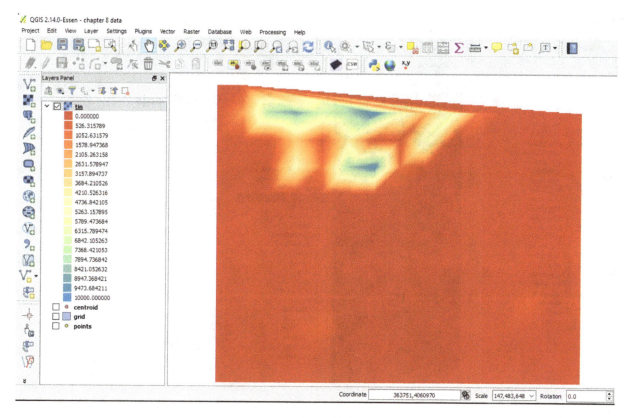

Figure 8.5:

I wanted more. I read a bit about 3D and QGIS. I had to load a plugin. I used the *Plugin Menu: Manage and Install Plugins*. I loaded `Qgis2threejs` (Figure 8.6, on the following page).

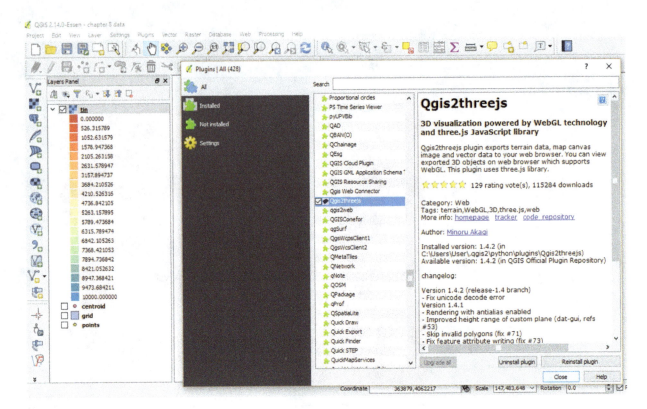

Figure 8.6:

Under *Web*, I selected the plugin and input 2 for the value of *World: Vertical Exaggeration*. Under *DEM* I selected my TIN layer. Under *Polygon*, I selected my Grid Layer. I browsed to a file location and named it **3d**. Then I clicked on *Run* (Figure 8.7, on the next page).

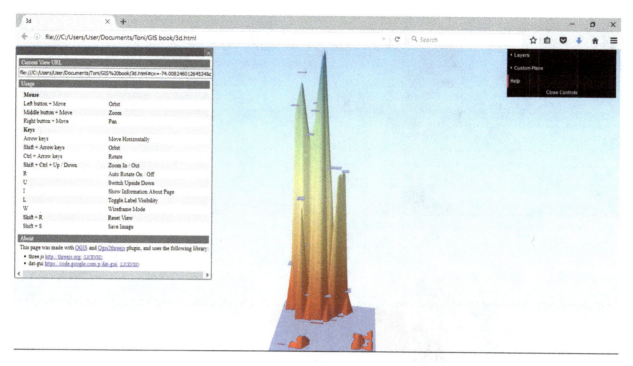

Figure 8.7:

I played around with the controls for a while to see what I could do, then saved the image. My files for the browser were saved as HTML files in the file manager so I could look at them again (Figure 8.8).

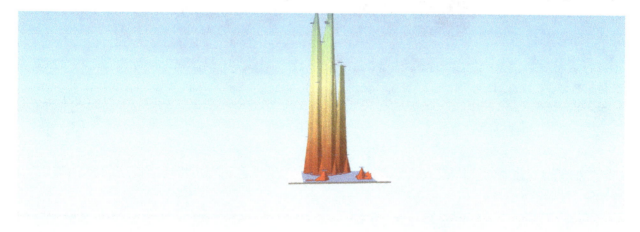

Figure 8.8:

I tried extruding the points from my grid to see what the effect would be. I thought it was even more interesting with the spheres on the pinnacles (Figure 8.9, on the next page and Figure 8.10, on page 97).

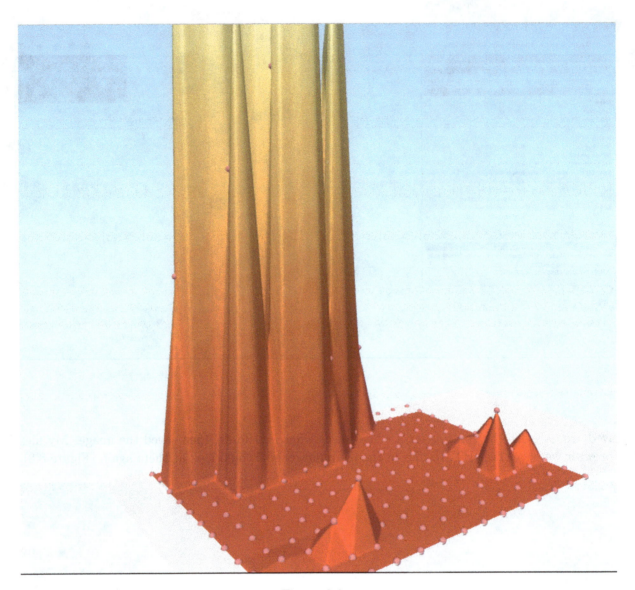

Figure 8.9:

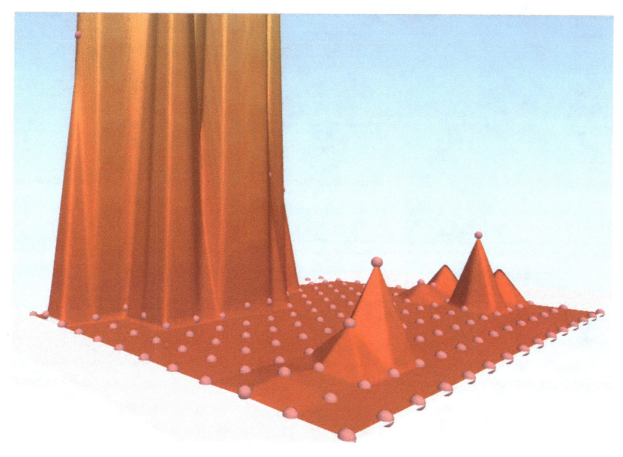

Figure 8.10:

I knew there was a lot more I could do with this to communicate how I felt about my world, to use qualitative GIS, but it was a start.

So many menus. So many possibilities. So much that could be done. It was like magic! And it was fun!

What would you map? How would you use the parameters? Can you make a 3D map that illustrates how you feel about your world?

9. Story Map

"Remember the invitations we made for my party?" I asked my friend.

"Yes, of course," she answered, taking another bite of her sandwich and wrinkling her nose. "I liked your mother's food a lot better than the stuff I get for lunch." She sighed and finished chewing her mouthful. "Why are you asking? Are you going to have another party?" she asked, looking sideways at me, hopefully.

"No. At least, not right now," I said, "That's not why I asked. "The teacher found out about the invitation idea I used for the party and the maps we made and she thought it was great. She asked me about it this morning before school and wondered if she could add onto the idea—wondered if I would mind."

"What did you say?"

"Of course I wouldn't mind, and I told the teacher so," I said. "I'm glad she liked the idea. Not that it will help me in school or anything," I added, hastily, in case my friend thought I was hunting for grades. "But it is nice to think someone thought I had a good idea."

"What do you think she wants to do with it?"

"Don't know," I answered.

We didn't have to wait long to find out. After lunch the teacher gave us a new assignment.

"Many of you made invitations recently, I understand," she began. There were looks of panic from the kids in the class who didn't want to come to my party and so didn't know how an invitation could be made. "No worries if you didn't, of course," she assured everyone. "There is lots of time to catch up and lots of people you can ask for help."

As if, I rolled my eyes at my friend—as if the elite clique would deign to ask the likes of me how to make an invitation using mapping software. Still, I would help anyone who asked. It never hurt to be kind and sometimes it really helped. When people were kind to me, I appreciated it immensely and never forgot.

"Here is what I would like you to do," she went on. "I understand you made maps of a place in the world where you came from. Or maps of where you might like to go, if your whole family was from our village, just so everyone would have something unique to make. This was just a great idea and we all know who we have to thank for it." She nodded at me and a few of my friends gave a little clap. Loudest clapping of all came from the new girl for whom I had given the party. I glowed and blushed in equal measures. My ears felt hot.

"I'd like to propose that we carry on with the same kind of idea, using something called a Story Map." She switched on the projector and typed *GIS Story Maps* into a browser search. Then she clicked on Images. She showed us some examples of story maps. "Have a look at these, if you like, for inspiration. Then I would like you to tell a story about the world using a map. Maybe a story about an explorer and the route they took. Maybe a story about an event you think is important. Maybe something about a famous person, an author, a composer, an artist. The point is, you decide what you want to tell about.

You decide how you can use a map to illustrate what you want to tell. You have two weeks. The week after next you will all get ten minutes to show your map and tell your story. Any questions?"

Lots of noise followed as people thought aloud and commented to their friends, then lots of hands started waving in the air.

"I know you have questions," our teacher said, "but I want you to think first. I don't want questions about the content of the map. I want that to come from you. I've given you a few ideas to think about. So, if your questions are about what to make your story about, put your hand down." Most of the hands dropped.

"Good," she said. "Now, for the other questions. Wait for a minute until I hand out the instructions for the end product. Then let's see if you still need some help." She started passing out the papers.

"Some of you will be good at making the map, some of you will be good at selecting a story to tell, some of you will be good at telling stories. All of us have different strengths. I want to see your strength. I want it to shine through. And," she paused, "I want to see your weaknesses too. It's okay not to be perfect, but it is a good idea to look at what you think you could have done better and to write about it. So, along with your map, I want you to write a few paragraphs about what you learned from making the Story Map. Think about what you wish you could have done better. Reflection, it's called. I want you to reflect on your work and on your product."

I read the instructions with some interest. The teacher wrote: *There are lots of ways to tell a story with pictures.*

1. One is to show a succession of pictures all at once, on one story board. To do this you could add four maps from the *Web : OpenLayers plugin*. You could *Zoom* to the different views that illustrate your story. Make one layer visible at a time by using the *Layers Panel* checkboxes (Figure 9.1, on the next page).

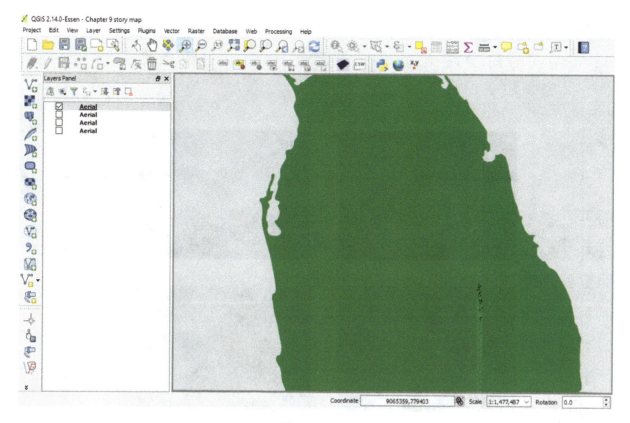

Figure 9.1:

Use *Project: New Print Composer*. Use the *Layout Menu: Add Map*. Draw a marquee for the first map. Repeat as many times as needed for each map that you need to show for your story (Figure 9.2, on the following page).

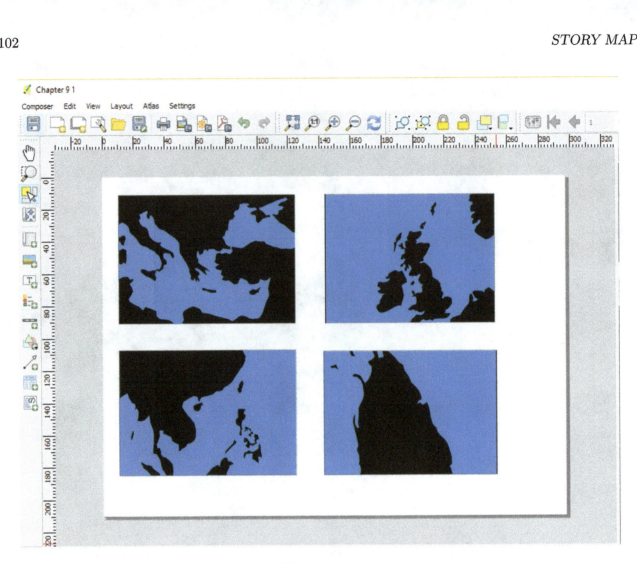

Figure 9.2:

2. Another way to tell a story is to use maps with bookmarks. Add a map from *Web: OpenLayers plugin*. Use the *View Menu: Show Bookmarks*. *Zoom* and use the hand to *Pan* the map until you have the location you want to use. On the *Spatial Bookmarks Panel*, click on the icon to *Add bookmark*. Name your bookmark. Repeat until you have your story mapped. Click on the appropriate bookmark to highlight it. On the *Spatial Bookmarks Panel*, click on the *Zoom to bookmark* (Figure 9.3, on the next page).

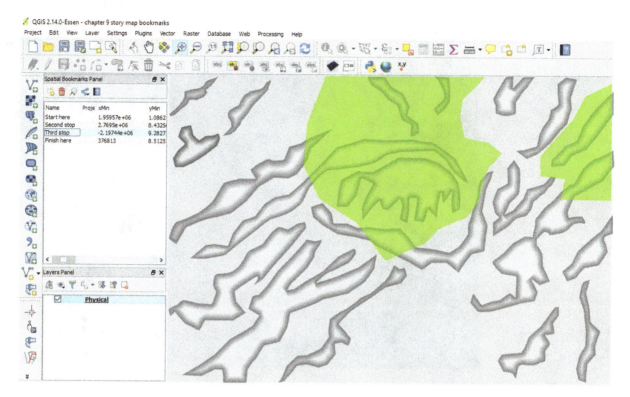

Figure 9.3:

3. Here is an example of revealing a route, perhaps the route used by Columbus. Use *Web: OpenLayers plugin* and add a map. Use *Layer: Create Layer: New Shapefile Layer*, type is line. Draw the line that shows the route traveled (Figure 9.4, on the following page).

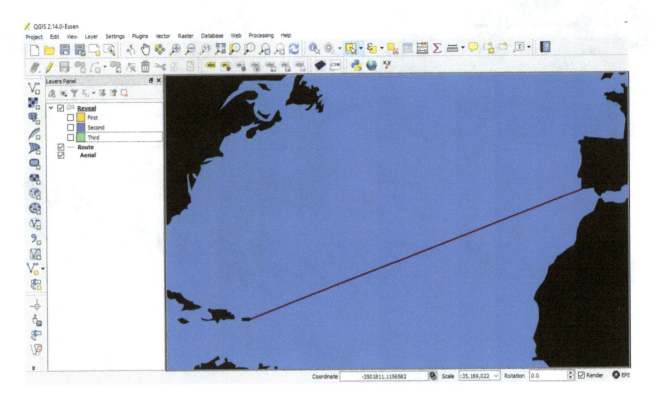

Figure 9.4:

Now create another *New Shapefile Layer*, type is polygon. *Add to fields list* a second field named `PolygonOrder`. Create three polygons covering the route so that as each part is made non-visible, a part of the route will be uncovered and you can talk about it. As you create them, name each polygon for a number in the part of the story: One, Two and Three, for example. Make the polygons touch, but not overlap—or as close as you can (Figure 9.5, on the next page).

Right click on the layer and select *Properties: Style: Categorized* by *PolygonOrder* so that each polygon will be a different colour. As you tell the story of the journey, you can reveal the journey parts. You could zoom into the start and end of the journey to show what the traveler saw (Figure 9.5, on the facing page and Figure 9.6, on the next page).

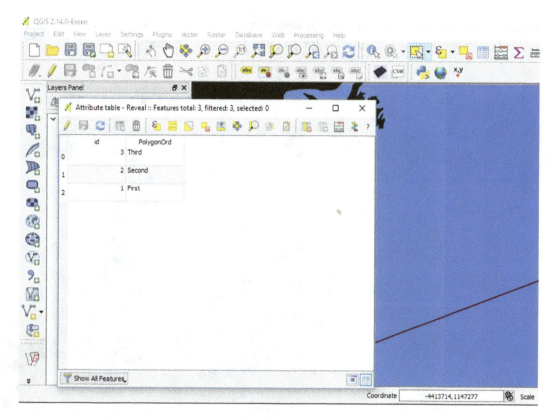

Figure 9.5:

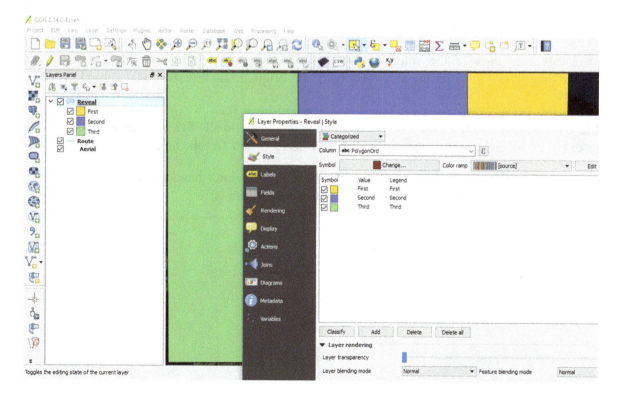

Figure 9.6:

You may want to add some labels to the map to help you remember how to tell your story. Use the Text Annotation Tool. It offers lots of possibilities for colours, fonts etc (Figure 9.7).

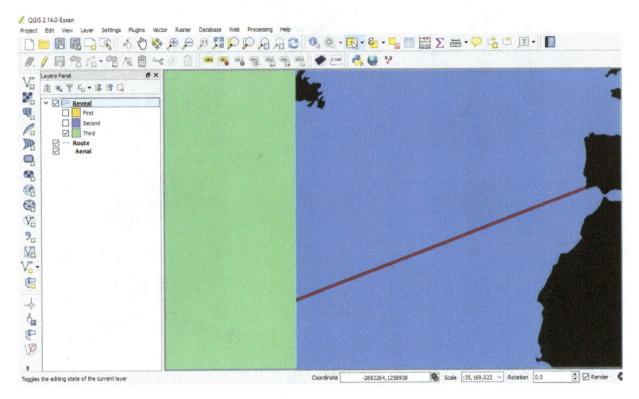

Figure 9.7:

These are only some ideas of how you could tell a story. Your story will help you decide how it needs to be told. Be daring. Tell an exciting story. Be bold. Be original. Be creative. Make mistakes, learn and HAVE FUN.

I read to the end of the instruction sheet. Okay, I thought, I can do all of those things. But first, I needed a story to tell. I needed to think about that before I decided how to tell the story using a map.

Do you already have an idea? What will you do with it? If you don't have an idea, how could you think of one? What story needs to be told? What's the best way to tell it?

10. GIS Quest Game

The Quest: Save the planet

In this activity, you are the creator of a GIS game. You will be provided with a story line and instructions to create a Quest game for a Player. Once the Player has played the game, they will have fulfilled the quest.

You will set up an opening view for the Player and instruct them on what they must do, which is to seek for and collect Rare Earths so that they can save the world and win the game.

The most important thing to remember is you are a winner if you learn something about GIS and the software. Don't worry if your results are not perfect, or are different from the steps and the screen captures, or what anyone else creates or does. Think of the steps below as suggestions, not rules. Being an explorer and trying out new things is the best way to learn. Making a game can be just as much fun as playing a game.

Part 1—Player's Manual

Here is the Player's Manual—the game setup consisting of the story and the instructions that the Player will read before they start playing.

The Story

I was standing on the marble stairs, pulling open the door to the science museum when I heard a ripping noise over my right shoulder. I turned to look. The air looked foggy, as though a cloud was between me and the railing of the stairs, even though the day was sunny. I heard a voice ordering me, "Take this", and a paper was thrust at me. I reached for it, just as the cloud cleared and the railing was once more visible.

I read the scrap of paper. "We need help! This message is from scientists in the year 2117. We need Rare Earths, but we can no longer get them. Climate change and environmental destruction have buried or destroyed them. Without the Rare Earths, we cannot save the world. Please, find them, save them from destruction so we will have access to them when our time comes. We will know you have the right Rare Earths if you have identified them by their correct colour. Do not fail! The world is counting on you!"

Well, that got my attention. I dropped the handle of the door to the museum and it eased shut in front of me. Rare Earths? Scientists from the future? What should I do? It didn't take me long to decide as I stood there in the street filled with car exhaust. I decided to take up the quest, but I will need your help.

Instructions

To find the Rare Earths, you will have to:

1. Use the Bookmark tool. Find Rare Earth One. Return to Aberdeen by book-mark. According to the instructions received, store Rare Earth One for safe keeping. To use the Bookmark Tool read the *QGIS User Guide, 8.12.2, Working with Bookmarks*.

2. After storing Rare Earth One, from Aberdeen, use the Zoom Out tool, *QGIS User Guide 8.6, Zooming and Panning* to find the next set of instructions for Rare Earth Two. Find the next set of instructions by changing symbology. Read about symbology, *QGIS User Guide 12.3*. The instructions will be invisible until you make them transparent by changing symbology. Once you have located Rare Earth Two, return to Aberdeen. Store it.

3. Use the Attribute Table to Zoom to Selected location, *QGIS User Guide 12.5, Working with the Attribute Table*. Locate and store Rare Earth Three.

> Okay, that was Part One, the part for the Players. Now we move on to the part for you, the creator of the game.

Part 2—Creating the Game

Outline of steps

Here are the steps you will follow to create the game:

A. Create an opening view.

B. Create a space for the Player where they store their work.

C. Create a place where they celebrate their win.

D. Create the Rare Earths at places in the world that the Player must find in their Quest and the instructions on how to follow the steps of the game.

Remember, you are in charge. You can make decisions about how to proceed and what to do! You can deviate from these instructions and change the game in any way you choose.

Warning! Making a computer game is complicated. People who are game developers love their work because it is so challenging. How will you tackle the challenge? Will you follow along and think about things while you do them. Will you follow along and wait to figure it out after you have finished? Will you read through and create a picture in your mind of how it all works? Will you read and make a diagram so that you can understand what is being done? Lots of strategies. What will you pick?

Create an opening view.

You will develop a game that Players will play to learn GIS. It will be a game of clues they will follow, using the instructions in their guide (described in Part One) and the QGIS manuals, to figure out how to access the clues and accumulate the Rare Earths. When they have succeeded in gathering the Rare Earths, they win.

Open QGIS and use the *Plugins Menu: Manage and Install Plugins: OpenLayers plugin*. Install it.

Use the *Web Menu: OpenLayers plugin* and select a satellite map. Use the *Zoom In and Pan Tools* to refresh the map if required to make it draw completely.

Use the *Plugins Menu: Manage and Install Plugins: Geosearch*. Install it. This plugin will allow you to find places in the world. You will use this to search for Aberdeen where the game will start. Once you are there, you want to create a bookmark so you can get back quickly from anywhere else in the world. Open the Geosearch Plugin from the Plugins Menu. Using the Point tab, type Aberdeen into the Address box. Click *Search*. Double click on the result to zoom to Aberdeen.

Look under the *View Menu: View: New Bookmark*. Add a new bookmark and name it Aberdeen. There is a tool on the Spatial Bookmarks Panel that looks like a magnifying glass. It is the *Zoom to bookmarks* tool. Your Player can use this to navigate around the world as the quest proceeds.

Aberdeen is the opening view for your game player.

Create a place where the Player will store their work.

Before you lead the player to their first clue to find the Rare Earths, think about the game's end. The Player will need a place to store their 'treasures', their Rare Earths, as they find them. You need to create a Vector Layer and name it 'Vault'. The Player will go to the Vault, as they acquire the Rare Earths, and leave them there.

1. Create the shapefile, Vault, using *Layer Menu: Create Layer: New Shapefile Layer*. The type will be polygon. Add a field with the *Name* Rare Earth. *Save* the shapefile with the name Vault.

2. Eventually, as you create them, there will be three polygons:

   - Promethium, Pm, pink
   - Europium, Eu, yellow
   - Thulium, Tm, grey.

3. When you create the polgyons, make sure they are not in the correct colour for the Rare Earths. As you will see, they need to be wrong to start so that the Player can correct the colours when they find the Rare Earths and return to the Vault to store them.

Create a space where the Player celebrates their win.

Once the Player has accumulated the Rare Earths, they 'win'. What do they get?

1. When the Player clicks from *QGIS GUI* to *Print Composer* view, everything changes. You will set up the *Print Composer* view so that it has the Rare Earth's Vault, the *Legend* showing the names and colours of the Rare Earths, and a message of congratulations for your winner. You might want to set it up as shown in Figure 10.1, on the next page. Use the *Project Menu: New Print Composer*.

2. Use the *Layout Menu: Add Map*, draw a rectangle. This will show the Rare Earths locations on the map.

3. Use the *Layout Menu: Add Label*. Type the text congratulating the Player. The *QGIS Training Manual, Chapter 5.1.3*, in *Creating Maps*, will help you with this. Notice that the text you placed

in the QGIS GUI is visible in the Print Composer View, but the text you put in the Print Composer View does not show up in the GUI View. The Composer View is like a secret; no one sees it until you tell them how to open it up.

4. Use the *Layout: Add Legend* and draw a box. This will show the Rare Earths and their colours. They can only have the correct colours if the Player has followed your instructions and found the Rare Earths.

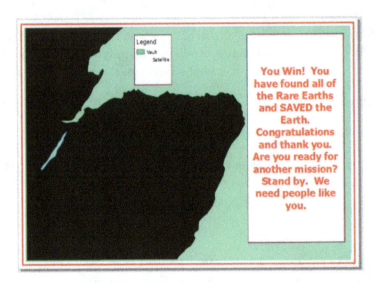

Figure 10.1:

Create the Rare Earths at places in the world that the Player must find in their quest.

The Quest: Rare Earth One

Now that you have set up the beginning and the end of the game, you need to set up the quest items, the Rare Earths, and the way in which the Player can find them. Game players need some easy wins to get started, then you can make it more difficult for them as they continue.

The *Bookmark* tool will be the first to be used, as it is easy to set up and use. Your game players will follow the bookmark to their first clue. Here are the steps:

1) First you are going to select a Rare Earth location.

2) Second, you are going to bookmark this location.

3) Third, you are going to create a new Polygon feature in the Vault Shapefile.

4) Fourth, you are going to create messages/instructions for the player at the Rare Earth Site.

5) Fifth, you are going to place a message at the Opening Scene of the game, Aberdeen, to tell the player how to go to the next Rare Earth.

1. Select a Rare Earth location.

Pan and Zoom In around on the map. Pick a place in the world for the Player to visit. Remember that the scientist has said that the Rare Earths have been destroyed by climate change or environmental destruction. Pick a place on a coast where it is likely that sea level rise will make the Rare Earths inaccessible.

2. Bookmark this location.

Use the *New Bookmark Tool* and call it Rare Earth 1 (or whatever you like).

3. Create a new polygon in the Vault Layer at this location.

At the bookmark location you have selected, Toggle on editing with the *Pencil Tool* and add a polygon to your shapefile. Type the name in the table, Promethium. *Save*. Right click on the layer. Select *Properties Style: Categorized*. Double click on the polygon for Prometheum and make it anything but pink. Remember, the Player must change it to pink, showing that the Rare Earth has been located and the Player knows the correct colour.

4. Create messages for the Player.

Click on the *Text Annotation* tool and type four messages in the text box to tell the Player to:

1. Make note of the name of the Rare Earth that is available here. This Rare Earth is pink.
2. Tell them to zoom back to Aberdeen using the bookmark tool.
3. Tell them how to change the symbology for the Rare Earth they have found (Right Click on Layer/Properties. Double click on symbol. Select colour, pink).
4. Tell them to look at the Instructions in their Player's Manual for how to find Rare Earth Two (Figure 10.2, on the following page).

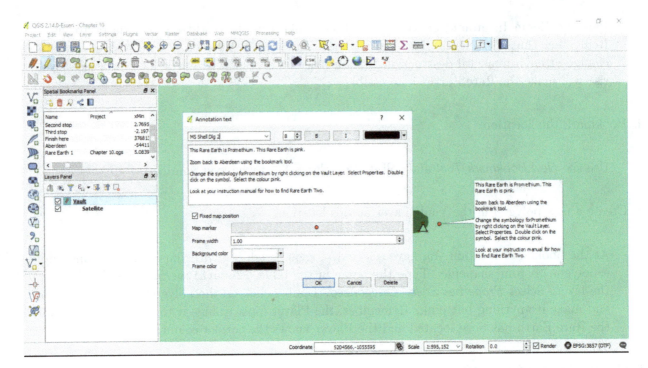

Figure 10.2:

Okay, that is one Rare Earth created and the instructions given on how to find it and place it in the vault. Now you need to do the same for two more Rare Earths. The player would get bored if it was just the same the second and third time, so you must give them more of a challenge each time.

The Quest: Rare Earth Two

1. You will create a hidden clue.

2. You will create interim clues.

3. You will create the polygon for Rare Earth Two.

1. Create a hidden clue.

Rare Earth one is stored. The Player is near Aberdeen. Remember Instruction 2 in the Player Manual? Instruction 2 tells them to use the Zoom Out tool and change symbology to transparent to find the next set of instructions for finding Rare Earth Two.

Create a Text Box, using the tool *Text Annotation*, out in the ocean near Aberdeen so they have to zoom out to find it. They will have to figure out how to make the colour transparent. They know how to do this by following Instruction 2, so you don't need to tell them how.

In the text box, type: *Use the Zoom to XY coordinates tool by installing the Plugins: Manage and Install Plugins: ZoomtoCoordinates to gain the location of the second Rare Earth site. Use these coordinates: -25532692, 6897561.*

Now, hide the message by making the background black. Note: This is just a suggestion, you can use any coordinates you like. The coordinates of your chosen location are at the bottom of the map, in the *Task Bar*. Copy and paste them to the message boxes you create in this and the next steps (Figure 10.3 and Figure 10.4).

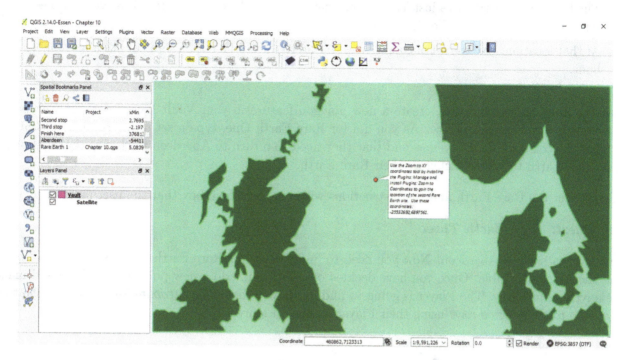

Figure 10.3:

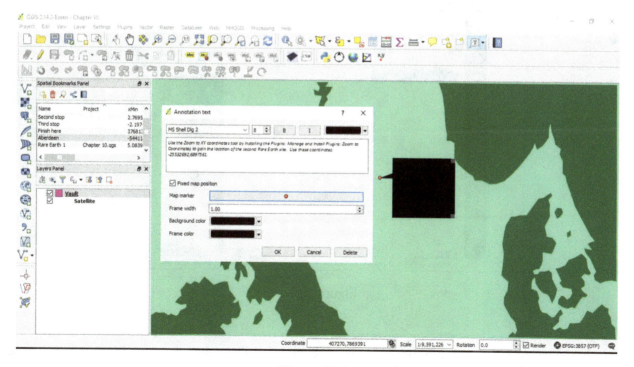

Figure 10.4:

2. Create interim clues so the Player has to search around before they get to the second Rare Earth site.

> The first set of coordinates just leads to another black text box. In that text box, give another set of coordinates to another location.
>
> At that location, give the set of coordinates to lead to the final location. Sort of like a scavenger hunt.

3. At the final, correct location, create a new polygon feature in your Vault Layer, name it Europeum and colour it anything but yellow. As you did for Rare Earth One, type a set of instructions to tell the user that the correct colour is yellow and that they need to return to Aberdeen to change the symbology of the Rare Earth to yellow and store their Rare Earth.

4. Cover over the Rare Earth and the instructions with another black box that the user must uncover.

The Quest: Rare Earth Three

The Player is back in Aberdeen. Now you need to find a place for Rare Earth Three so they can find it using the Attribute Table. Once you have decided on a location, add a new polygon, Thulium and make it be anything but grey. The Player is going to find out how to open the *Attribute Table* and use the tool *Zoom map to the selected rows* using their Player manual (Figure 10.5).

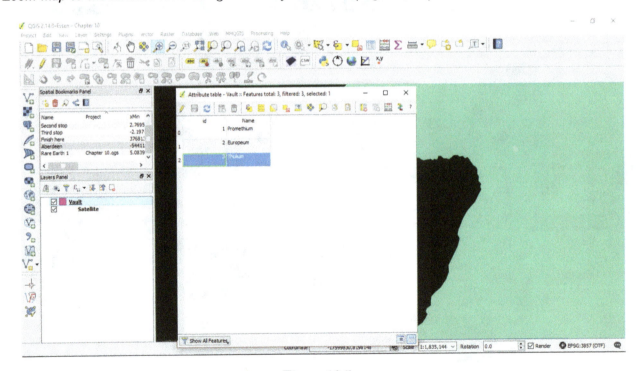

Figure 10.5:

Leave the following instructions at the location of Thulium. "The colour is grey. Store it in the vault. Now use the File: Print Composers. Click on the Composer associated with this project to find out what happens next."

They have succeeded! They have three Rare Earths for the Scientist, the vault is now complete and have received their final, congratulatory message from the scientists of the future (Figure 10.6).

Figure 10.6:

More?

Play it through. See if it works correctly. What can you do to make it better, more exciting?

Want to create a Part Two? Explore some tools and plugins. Watch some QGIS videos on YouTube. What would the story be? What ways to explore and find could you discover to show to your Player? The software is there and it has hundreds of tools, you just need to know how to use the tools to set up the "hide and seek." Playing games is fun but making them is even more fun!

11. Mission Accomplished

I heard the alarm clock, but I cuddled the blankets tight under my chin. Our house was freezing. It felt like winter was here already, but everyone said it wouldn't really get stuck in until the end of December. I wondered what it would be like then. Could I survive those temperatures? In this drafty old house? My room was Antarctica. The bathroom was the North Pole and, no, I did not enjoy playing polar bear in the bath even if my Mum thought it was a funny idea.

The kitchen was lots warmer now that the old stove had been replaced with a fancy new stone stove, the kind that stayed on all day and you could lean against to keep warm. Come to think of it, if I just got my uniform on and ran for the stairs, I could warm up by the stove. The thought was enough to galvanize me to action. I sprang. A deer could have done no better. Then I leapt like a rabbit, flew like a bird down the stairs. Polar bears. Way too slow. She had to be kidding, only the swift could survive in this house.

We'd been in our new house for three months now. There had been lots of changes. In the beginning, the house seemed overwhelming. The rooms behind the doors had been a mystery to us, but now they had been explored and mapped. Not that we had completed our discoveries or our learning about the things they held. That nest of mice last week, hiding in the back of one of the unused bedroom closets certainly made us jump a bit when they went running every which way. And the massive leak in the attic was an interesting discovery when it made itself known to us through the collapse of the ceiling over my parent's dressing table. Yes, there was still work to be done.

Meanwhile, my Dad had taken over the kitchen and the library. They were organised and redecorated. I'm like my Dad. He likes colour. As paint colours, Raspberry and Mango go really well together—who would have guessed. And my Mum, well, she's worked hard designing the studio space she needs as well as drawing up plans for the garden which I am sure we will all be working on in the spring. I like flowers, but I wish there wasn't so much shoveling involved in growing them. Sometimes I wish we had some garden gnomes. But, no, only hard work would bring the rewards. I would have to inure myself to that.

When I got to the kitchen, still wearing, yes, you remember, my ugly grey uniform, I sprinted to the stove and leaned against it gratefully. Mum, Dad, and my little brother were already at the table. "Toast?" asked Dad.

"Yes, please."

"Ready for a scintillating new day at school?" Mum asked encouragingly, as she did every day.

"Actually, it is going to be a good day," I said. They looked surprised and then interested. That was not my usual answer. Usually I only grunted a bit so they wouldn't ask any more questions.

"Today we are going to present the work we have been doing all term in our mapping program."

"Oh, yes, that's QGIS, right?" Mum said. I had showed her the program and she had actually used it to draw some plans for the garden. "That's a great tool. What are you going to present?"

"The teacher has divided us into groups. One group is going to present data, explaining Rasters and Vectors."

"What?" said my little brother. He heard words alien to his ears, but he was really more interested in dipping the toes of his plastic figures into the jam on his toast, so I ignored him.

"Another group is going to talk about Coordinate Reference Systems. There's one about Qualitative Data versus Quantitative Data and about ways to Classify Data. And there's a presentation on Digital Terrain Models."

"Sounds like interesting stuff," said Dad, looking impressed with the jargon I was throwing around. And I wasn't even showing off. I really did know what all of the things meant. I had learned! And I was quite proud of myself.

"I'm going to talk about Concept Maps. We each made our own as we worked through our lessons, recording and linking new concepts as we learned them. My teacher picked her favourite Concept Maps from the class. She liked mine because of the bright colours I used. I put a border all around my Concept Maps from each chapter, showing how my final map had evolved. Here, I'll show you." I left the comfort of the stove and walked to my book bag, hanging on the hook by the kitchen door. I brought out my binder and opened it to the page with my printed Concept Map.

"Wow," said my Dad. "That is bright. Great colours. Looks Equatorial. I love it! Why be dull and dreary. . ."

"When you can be bright and cheery," I finished the old joke and he laughed as he always does.

"It is lovely, dear," said my Mum. "Looks very busy. If you learned all those terms, I'm impressed."

"My teacher said that GIS is a good learning platform. It teaches us how to communicate information and how to analyse data and that's only the start. The program we have, QGIS, is Open Source. She says if we are good at using it, any one of us could contribute to its development. We could write a Plugin and if it was good enough, it could be added to the program for everyone to use. She says we don't just have to be users of software, we can shape it too."

"Is that like creating an App?" my brother asked, putting his jammy toy down on the table, finally hearing something that he was interested in. "Can you make lots of money?" He and his friends had recently been enamored of the idea of getting rich by selling on the Internet.

"I guess it is kind of like an App," I said, "but it goes inside the program—it isn't just for download off the web. And, no, you can't get rich, its Open Source. That means people create things and share them. Nobody gets paid and nobody pays."

"Open source is a great thing," my Mum said. "Think of our garden. If I do it all alone, it could take years to get it done. But with everyone's help, we'll all be able to enjoy it much sooner. And we all get practice at gardening. People who contribute and help in Open Source, get practice at developing solutions and get to use what others have developed as well."

"Think of it this way," added my Dad. "If a company pays 100 people to solve a problem, they might be lucky and get 100 possible solutions, and will implement one, but with the Open Source community, tens of thousands of people can look at a problem that needs to be solved and not only will there likely be a great solution, but there will be multiple solutions of all different kinds. People can choose which one they want to use."

"There's lots of reasons to be a part of the Open Source community," continued my Mum. "Wanting to help, wanting to give back, caring about making things better for everyone."

I understood what my parents were saying, but I could tell my brother was not quite convinced. Still, he did take a quick look at my Concept Map. And, after all, he was my little brother, so I suppose I probably should care about his development and take the time to show him the program. I looked at his jam covered face. Later, I thought. When I was feeling beneficent, perhaps. Was there a Be Kind to Little Brother's day in the not too near future?

Glossary of Terms

Active Layer:

Only one layer is active at a time. When the layer is clicked on, it is highlighted and becomes active so that you can work with it. See Layer.

Active Learning:

Having someone tie your shoes for you is easy. If you remember learning how to tie them you probably remember being frustrated. It wasn't easy! Similarly, having someone tell you the answer or tell you what and how to think, is easy while reading, exploring, investigating, researching and being responsible for your own learning is hard. But will there always be someone there to tie your shoes for you? No. Do you want there always to be someone there to tell you how and what to think? Learning how to learn is an important part of active learning and it takes practice to get good at it. Sometimes the more difficult the task, the more challenging it is, the more fun it can be to accomplish it. Active learning can be frustrating, it can be challenging, but it can be fun as well. It is student centred, it is all about you!

Active Tool:

Only one tool is active at a time. The Active Tool is highlighted. On the map, the cursor becomes an image of the icon that is active. To select another tool, click on the tool and it will become active, while the formerly selected tool deactivates. It is a good idea to check which tool is active before clicking on the map. See Tools.

Annotation:

The text on maps. Text annotation can be added using the icon in the QGIS GUI or using the Label in QGIS Print Composer.

Attribute Table:

The maps are what we usually look at in a GIS, but the tables are what cause the maps to be drawn. Data can be created in a GIS by digitizing onto the map. What is drawn is converted into data in an attribute table which stores the location of points, or the points along a line or of the boundaries of a polygon. For example, an attribute table of a point shapefile for Cities, will contain the location of the city as an X,Y coordinate and could also hold attributes of the elements which describe them: a field for Name, Population, and Size, if you add the fields. See Field.

Bookmark:

A saved location viewed at a specific scale that can be retrieved.

Buffer:

A Buffer is an area around a feature that is calculated based on the distance specified from the feature. Buffers are polygons. They can be drawn around points, lines or polygons.

Centroid:

The middle of a polygon.

Classifying Data:

Maps are a form of communication. We want our maps to communicate information clearly and in an easy way for the user to interpret. If we simply put all kinds of numbers on a map, it wouldn't be easy for a reader to use, but if we group the numbers into a few classes, for example, 0–10, 10–20, and 20 and above, and use colours or size to illustrate the different classes, it is much easier to see. Sometimes we know what we want to show, sometimes we need to explore methods to uncover what the data holds. Sometimes the data is limited and can only be displayed using certain methods. There are many different ways to group, or classify information and they depend on the data and the intent of the person creating the map.

Concept Map:

A Concept Map is a way to display information using a graphic representation. Concept Maps can organise information, structure thought, indicate potential new relationships, and integrate old and new information. Looking online at images of Concept Maps is a good way to understand how they work and what can be done, but your Concept Map is uniquely your own and is an illustration of what you think is important about a particular concept.

Coordinate Reference System:

Coordinate Reference System are geographic or projected. Geographic systems represent the world as a globe and use latitude and longitude in degrees, minutes and seconds, or decimal degrees. Projected systems represent the world in two dimensions, like a paper map, which stretches and distorts shape, area, distance, or direction. The use of the map dictates the choice of the projection so as to preserve the most important characteristics. A popular choice of projection is the Universal Transverse Mercator in which the X coordinate is represented with six numbers (called an Easting) and the Y coordinate by seven (known as Northing). See X, Y Coordinate.

Digital Elevation Model:

A DEM is made of cells and is a Raster. It is important to note that this is a model of the elevation. Models are approximations of reality. Each cell of data has a height (usually called a Z value) associated with it, as is captured by a satellite or airplane flying over the location. Sometimes used synonymously with DTM. See Digital Terrain Model and Raster.

Digital Terrain Model:

A DTM is made of points and/or lines and is a vector elevation model. It is important to note that this is a model of the elevation. Models are approximations of reality. Each point of data has a height (usually called a Z value) associated with it, as is captured by a satellite or airplane flying over the location. Sometimes used synonymously with DEM. See Digital Elevation Model.

Digitize:

To digitally draw or trace.

Feature:

One element of a Layer, either vector or raster. Features can be added, moved, identified, selected, and deleted using tools. See Layer, Vector, Raster, and Active Tool.

Field:

A field is a part of a table, also called an Attribute Table. Depending on the program, fields may also be called columns. Each field has only one type of data in it which can be text (also known as string), numerical (integer or real), or date. A text field can accept numbers, but a numeric field cannot accept text. Be sure to set the field type correctly for the attributes you need to store. See Attribute Table.

GIS:

Geographic Information System. A GIS is a system that works with spatial data, to store, manipulate, display, and analyse. It's more than just a digital map. It's a database with topology, meaning that each data element knows where it is in relation to other elements. As with any database, the data can be queried, and, since GIS has spatial characteristics, it can be queried about what it is and where it is. GIS started in the 1960's, but did not become mainstream until recently. Now we use online GIS web maps all the time to plan our trips and to find locations without really knowing much about the GIS that is working in the background. Knowing more about GIS may help us to make more fully informed decisions about our world.

Group Work:

Working together as a group in school paves the way for working as a team in jobs. From the amount of literature available and the number of companies that offer services to businesses on how to develop effective teams, it would appear that we don't always learn how to work as a group very effectively while we are in school and we still need help with it when we start to work. Why is that? Do you think groups or teams most often fail because they don't know what they are supposed to do, because they don't know how to do it, or because they can't/don't communicate with each other? Or is it a combination of all three? Do you think learning to work as a team before starting the work the team needs to do is a good idea? If you are interested in more about team work, search online for Belbin's Team Roles and find out what kind of team player you are.

GUI:

Graphic User Interface. The icons, menus, and elements that display on the computer screen and respond to being clicked by the mouse.

Interpolation:

The estimated value between known values.

Layer:

GIS organises information by type. If the element of the world can be modeled as a point, such as the location of a tree, then all of the points that represent trees can be put into one file. When this file is displayed in the GIS, it is called a layer. Other layers will represent other files of different kinds, such as polygons for lakes or lines for roads. Layers have a display order, with the topmost layer drawing onto the display last, so that it draws on the top of all of the other layers. The layer is only a pointer to the data. It is not the data itself. If you move the location of the data on your computer, the layer will no longer draw. See Active Layer.

Layout:

A layout consists of a map or maps and marginalia (information about the map) such as the scale, legend, title, author, date, and projection. The Print Composer holds the Layout.

Pan:

To move to a different area of the map while staying at the same scale. See Zoom in, Zoom out, and Scale.

Plugin:

Plugins provide additional functionality. They are accessed via the Plugin Menu, Manage and Install Plugins. Plugins used in this book are: *Open Layers Plugin, Geosearch, Zoom to Coordinates, Azimuth and Distance*, and *Qgis23js*.

Project:

A Project is a workspace that is created and can be saved as a .qgs file. It holds Layers and the properties that have been saved for them as well as Print Composer files of map layouts. Anything you do within a Project can be saved and will be retrieved when the Project is reopened.

Projection:

See X, Y Coordinate and Coordinate Reference System.

Property:

Layers have properties. Double clicking on the Layer brings up the layer properties. Right clicking on a Layer brings up a menu list, one of which is properties. The types of properties for a Layer are dependent on the kind of Layer it is. Different Layer properties allow for alternative ways to display data including such things as labeling and symbology (colour, size etc.), and will detail the location of the file on your computer that is being referenced by the Layer file. See Layer and Active Layer.

Pseudo colour:

Pseudo means false, so pseudo colour is false colour. In a raster image, each cell has a different number, from 0 to 255, which maps to a colour for a colour image, or to gradations of grey for a black and white image. To make the gradations of grey more apparent in a black and white image, pseudo colour can be used.

QGIS:

An Open Source GIS that can be used free of charge. Open Source software is developed and supported by a worldwide community of users who are dedicated to providing a complete, user friendly alternative to commercial software. In 2011, it is estimated there were 100,000 users of QGIS worldwide.

Qualitative Research:

Qualitative data is not quantifiable. It relies on descriptions, not numbers. Sample sizes for the research are small. Researchers do not know what they will find when they begin; they seek to uncover information. The studies are not generalizable; they cannot be used to describe larger populations. The researchers are interpreters and observers.

Quantitative Research:

Quantitative data involves numbers. This is the kind of research most commonly associated with science. Researchers start with a hypothesis. The studies use statistical methods and rely on large, random samples. It is hoped that findings can be used to describe larger populations or events.

Raster:

Raster data is a way of modeling the world using a grid of equal sized cells in rows and columns. It is considered a continuous method of data representation and is the alternative to Vector data. Every part of the map is filled with data, for continuous coverage, not just parts of it as is the case in Vector's discrete representation. Each cell can only represent one value, so the size of the grid's cells is extremely important. The size of the cell represents the raster's resolution. Whatever fills the majority of the cell is what gets represented. If one cell has a house in 75% of the cell and trees in 25%, then you won't see trees in that cell. If you zoom in closely to a photo from your mobile or digital camera, you will see the cells of the raster, called pixels (short for picture elements). See Vector.

Render:

How something draws or displays.

Scale:

Map scale is a representative fraction. A map of 1/2000 (or 1:2000) means that 1 unit on the map represents 2000 units on the ground. A map of 1/20,000 (1:20000) means that 1 unit on the map represents 20,000 units on the ground. Considered as a fraction, one 2000th is larger than one 20,000th which is why a 1:2000 map is a larger scale map and a 1:20,000 map is a smaller scale map.

Shapefile:

A format for saving digital data representing points, lines and polygons with a special attribute that stores location. The shapefile will appear as one layer in a GIS, but is made of several files stored on the computer, .dbf, .shx, .prj, and .shp. All files must be present and in the same location for the shapefile to be functioning. Shapefiles can be created (Create New Shapefile Layer) and can be added (Add Vector Layer) to one or to multiple projects. To add a shapefile that has already been created, browse to the file location and select the .shp file. See Layer.

Symbology:

The ways that data can be visualised including such elements as size and colour of font; colour, pattern and outline for polygons; or thickness, colour and pattern for lines. Symbology is an important part of cartography which assists with communicating information through maps and is both a science and an art.

Tools:

Tools are icons on the GUI. Tools are organized into toolbars. Hovering the cursor over a tool will reveal the name of the tool. See GUI and Active Tool.

Triangulated Irregular Network:

A TIN is a vector data set and is a kind of Digital Terrain Model. Points with X, Y, and Z values are used to create a TIN. X and Y represent location and Z represents elevation. The points become the vertices of triangles of varying sizes and shapes. The triangles don't overlap. See X, Y Coordinates and Digital Terrain Model.

Vector:

Vector data is a way of modeling the world using points, lines, and polygons. It is considered a discrete method of data representation. Depending on scale, rivers are lines or polygons and cities are points or polygons. Vector data is good for boundaries and locations of non-natural elements. Coastlines and swamps can be mapped with vectors, but exact representation of water levels will always be problematic. Imagine standing at the edge of a wetland, how wet do your feet have to be before it has ceased being land and started to be swamp? See Raster.

X, Y coordinate:

On a coordinate grid, X represents the horizontal and Y represents the vertical. For latitude and longitude, X represents the longitude and Y the latitude. As the cursor moves over the map, the coordinates are shown in the Status Bar at the bottom of the map. Sometimes X, Y coordinates also have a Z value associated with them representing elevation. See Coordinate Reference System and Digital Terrain Model.

Zoom in:

To change the view of the map display to a larger scale map while staying in the same area. See Zoom in, Pan, and Scale.

Zoom out:
 To change the view of the map display to a smaller scale map while staying in the same area. See Zoom out, Pan, and Scale.

Supplementary Reading

Constructivism

Brooks, M. & Brooks, J. (1999). The courage to be constructivist. *The constructivist classroom*, 57 (3). http://www.ascd.org/publications/educational-leadership/nov99/vol57/num03/The-Courage-to-Be-Constructivist.aspx

Educational Broadcasting Corporation (2004). Constructivism as a paradigm for teaching and learning. *Concept to classroom*. Available online: http://www.thirteen.org/edonline/concept2class/constructivism/index.html

Fosnot, C. (2005). *Constructivism: theory, perspectives and practice*. New York: Teachers College Press.

Jonassen, D. (1994). Thinking technology: Toward a constructivist design model, *Educational Technology*, 3.

Richardson, V. (ed). (1997). *Constructivist teacher education: Building a world of new understandings*. New York: Routledge.

Steffe, L. & Gale, J. (2012). *Constructivism in education*. New York: Routledge.

Concept Mapping

Jonassen, D. (2006). *Modeling with technology*. New Jersey: Pearson Education.

Jonassen, D. (2006). On the role of concepts in learning and instructional design. *Educational Technology Research and Development*, 54 (2).

Jonnassen, D., Howland, J., Marra, R., & Crismond, D. (2008). *Meaningful learning with technology*. New Jersey: Pearson.

Novak, J. (2005). Results and implications of a 12-Year longitudinal study of science concept learning. *Research in Science Education*, 35.

Novak, J. & Canas, A. (2006). The origins of the concept mapping tool and the continuing evolution of the tool. *Information Visualization Journal*, 5 (3).

University of Waterloo Centre for Teaching Excellence (nd). Concept Mapping Tools. Available at: https://uwaterloo.ca/centre-for-teaching-excellence/teaching-resources/teaching-tips/educational-technologies/all/concept-mapping-tools

Storytelling

Hutchens, D. (2015). *Circle of the 9 muses: A storytelling field guide for innovators and meaning makers*. New Jersey: Wiley.

Hsu, J. (2008). The secrets of storytelling. *Scientific American Mind*, 19.

Masse, C., Pounds, K., Church, E., Waters, R. & Souders, V. (2015). Story for learning and gaming. *Design and development of training games: Practical guidelines from a multidisciplinary perspective.* Hussain, T. & Coleman, S. (eds). New York: Cambridge University Press.

Shepard, C. (2015). *Seven ways in which stories power learning.* Available online: `http://clive-shepherd.blogspot.co.uk/2015/02/seven-ways-in-which-stories-power.html`

Shepard, C. (2015). *Compelling content hooks you in and won't let go.* Available online: `http://clive-shepherd.blogspot.co.uk/2015/08/compelling-content-hooks-you-in-and.html`

Books from Locate Press

QGIS Map Design

USE QGIS TO TAKE YOUR CARTOGRAPHIC PRODUCTS TO THE HIGHEST LEVEL.

With step-by-step instructions for creating the most modern print map designs seen in any instructional materials to-date, this book covers everything from basic styling and labeling to advanced techniques like illuminated contours and dynamic masking.

See how QGIS is rapidly surpassing the cartographic capabilities of any other geoware available today with its data-driven overrides, flexible expression functions, multitudinous color tools, blend modes, and atlasing capabilities. A prior familiarity with basic QGIS capabilities is assumed. All example data and project files are included.

Written by two of the leading experts in the realm of open source mapping, Anita and Gretchen are experienced authors who pour their wealth of knowledge into the book. Get ready to bump up your mapping experience!

The PyQGIS Programmer's Guide

EXTENDING QGIS JUST GOT EASIER!

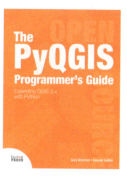

This book is your fast track to getting started with PyQGIS. After a brief introduction to Python, you'll learn how to understand the QGIS Application Programmer Interface (API), write scripts, and build a plugin. The book is designed to allow you to work through the examples as you go along. At the end of each chapter you'll find a set of exercises you can do to enhance your learning experience.

The PyQGIS Programmer's Guide is compatible with the version 2.0 API released with QGIS 2.x. All code samples and data are freely available from the book's website. Get started learning PyQGIS today!

Geospatial Power Tools

EVERYONE LOVES POWER TOOLS!

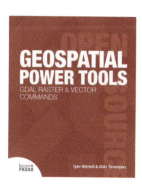

The GDAL and OGR apps are the power tools of the GIS world—best of all, they're free.

The utilities include tools for examining, converting, transforming, building and analysing data. This book is a collection of the GDAL and OGR documentation, but also includes new content designed to help guide you in using the utilities to solve your current data problems.

Inside you'll find a quick reference for looking up the right syntax and example usage quickly. The book is divided into three parts: *Workflows and examples*, *GDAL raster utilities*, and *OGR vector utilities*.

Once you get a taste of the power the GDAL/OGR suite provides, you'll wonder how you ever got along without them.

Discover QGIS

GET MAPPING WITH DISCOVER QGIS!

Get your hands on the award winning GeoAcademy exercises in a convenient workbook format. The GeoAcademy is the first ever GIS curriculum based on a national standard—the U.S. Department of Labor's Geospatial Competency Model—a hierarchical model of the knowledge, skills, and abilities needed to work as a GIS professional in today's marketplace.

The GeoAcademy material in this workbook has been updated for use with QGIS v2.14, Inkscape v0.91, and GRASS GIS v7.0.3. This is the most up-to-date version of the GeoAcademy curriculum. To aid in learning, all exercise data includes solution files.

The workbook is edited by one of the lead GeoAcademy authors, Kurt Menke, a highly experienced FOSS4G educator.

See these books and more at http://locatepress.com

www.ingramcontent.com/pod-product-compliance
Lightning Source LLC
Chambersburg PA
CBHW060153060326
40690CB00018B/4090